The Caregiver's Companion

Readings and Professional Resources

Janet Gonzalez-Mena

Napa Valley College

Connect
Learn
Succeed™

The Caregiver's Companion: Readings and Professional Resources
to accompany
INFANTS, TODDLERS, AND CAREGIVERS: A CURRICULUM OF RESPECTFUL,
RESPONSIVE, AND RELATIONSHIP-BASED CARE AND EDUCATION
Janet Gonzalez-Mena

Published by McGraw-Hill Higher Education, an imprint of The McGraw-Hill Companies, Inc., 1221
Avenue of the Americas, New York, NY 10020. Copyright © 2012, 2009, and 2007 by The McGraw-Hill
Companies, Inc. All rights reserved. Printed in the United States of America.

2 3 4 5 6 7 8 9 0 QDB/QDB 1 0 9 8 7 6 5 4 3 2

ISBN: 978-0-07-749035-5
MHID: 0-07-749035-5

www.mhhe.com

Contents

Part 1. Readings 1
Section 1 Chapter Readings

Chapter 1, Principles, Practice, and Curriculum
Reading 1 Caring for Infants with Respect: The RIE Approach 5
MAGDA GERBER

Chapter 2, Infant-Toddler Education
Reading 2 Curriculum and Lesson Planning: A Responsive Approach 11
J. RONALD LALLY

Chapter 3, Caregiving as Curriculum
Reading 3 Respectful, Individual, and Responsive Caregiving for Infants 15
BEVERLY KOVACH AND DENISE DA ROS

Chapter 4, Play as Curriculum
Reading 4 Faciltating the Play of Children at Loczy 21
ANNA TARDOS

Chapter 5, Attachment
Reading 5 A Primary Caregiving System for Infants and Toddlers: Best for Everyone Involved 25
JENNIFER L. BERNHARDT

Chapter 6, Perception
Reading 6 Excerpt from Our Moving Bodies Tell Stories, Which Speak of Our Experiences 33
SUZI TORTORA, ZERO TO THREE, MAY 1004, PAGES 5-6

Chapter 7, Motor Skills
Reading 7 The Development of Movement 37
EMMI PIKLER

Chapter 8, Cognition
Reading 8 How Infants and Toddlers Use Symbols 43
KAREN MILLER

Chapter 9, Language
Reading 9 Preparing for Literacy: Communication Comes First 47
RUTH ANNE HAMMOND

Chapter 10 Emotions
Reading 10 Helping a Baby Adjust to Center Care 51
ENID ELLIOT

Chapter 11 Social Skills
Reading 11 Toddlers: What to Expect 59
JANET GONZALEZ-MENA

Chapter 12 The Physical Environment
Reading 12 Creating a Landscape for Learning 65
LOUIS TORELLI AND CHARLES DURRETT

Chapter 13 The Social Environment
Reading 13 The Impact of Child Care Policies and Practices on
Infant/Toddler Idenity Formation. 69
J. RONALD LALLY

Chapter 14 Adult Relations In Infant-Toddler Care and Education Programs
Reading 14 Cross Cultural Conferences 73
JANET GONZALEZ-MENA

Section 2: Overarching Themes
Readings on Health and Safety
Reading 15 Sudden Infant Death Syndrome: Ask Dr. Sue Your Health and Safety Questions 81
SUSAN S. ARONSON

Reading 16 Supporting the Development of Infants and Toddlers with Special Health Needs 83
CYNTHIA HUFFMAN

Reading 17 Breastfeeding Promotion in Child Care 89
LAURA DUTIL AIRD

Readings on Culture and Families
Reading 18 Cultural Dimensions of Feeding Relationships 95
CAROL BRUNSON PHILLIPS AND RENATTA COOPER

Reading 19 Cultural Differences in Sleeping Practices 103
JANET GONZALEZ-MENA AND NAVAZ PESHOTAN BHAVNAGRI

Readings on Including Infants and Toddlers with Special Needs
Reading 20 Talking with Parents When Concerns Arise. 109
LINDA BRAULT AND JANET GONZALEZ-MENA

Reading 21 Strategies for Supporting Infants and Toddlers with
Disabilities in Inclusive Child Care. 117
DONNA SULLIVAN AND JANET GONZALEZ-MENA

Part II. Important Forms 125

Part III. Communicating with Parents 149

Part IV. Observation 155
Observation Guidelines 157
Video Observations 159

The Caregiver's Companion

Introduction

What you have in your hands are supplemental readings and resources to enhance your understanding and use of the material in *Infants, Toddlers, and Caregivers*. This companion is organized into four parts. First are the readings themselves, which are divided into two sections. Section One, Chapter Readings, goes chapter-by-chapter, offering one article that corresponds to each chapter of the textbook. Part II, Important Forms, includes numerous forms that can be used in infant-toddler programs. Part III, Communicating with Parents, provides an outline of a parent hand-book followed by sample letters and notices that could be included in the handbook. Part IV, Observation, includes guidelines for observing followed by Video Observations related to the video clips for each chapter of the text found at the book's Online Learning Center at http://www.mhhe.com/itc9e. The goal of the Companion Manual is to give you more resources and support for the practical application of the material in *Infants, Toddlers, and Caregivers*.

—Janet Gonzalez-Mena

Part I

Readings Related to *Infants, Toddlers, and Caregivers*

Section 1: Chapter readings

Section 2: Overarching Themes
    Readings on Health and Safety
    Readings on Culture and Families
    Readings on Including Infants and
    Toddlers with Special Needs

Section 1

Chapter Readings

Chapter 1

Principles, Practice, and Curriculum

As you read Chapter 1 of your text, notice how this article corresponds to the 10 principles. You'll see a different style of writing and perhaps hear a different voice, because this article was written by Magda Gerber herself, about her philosophy. This article about respect comes straight from her. As you read it, compare the information and the tone to Chapter 1. See if you can discern the similarities. Do you also perceive some differences?

Reading 1

Caring for Infants with Respect: The RIE Approach

by Magda Gerber, M.A.

Magda Gerber, M.A., has been a child therapist, lecturer, and consultant on infant care. For many years she was an associate of Emmi Pikler, M.D. in Budapest, Hungary, and was director and co-founder, with Tom Forrest, M.D., of Resources for Infant Educators in Los Angeles, California. She taught at Pacific Oaks College in Pasadena, California, and has applied her theories to normal as well as high-risk infants in several California infant programs.

Walking into a RIE workshop for new mothers and infants, you might encounter the following scene:

Five mothers sit quietly observing their infants in the adjacent play area. One baby has discovered a multi-colored ball, filled with just enough air for his palmar grasping skill. Another infant sits quietly, looking pensively at her reflection in the dome of an upside-down aluminum mixing bowl. Two adults sit attentively among the infants. One 8 month old baby approaches another with outstretched fingers, heading toward an open eye. One of the adults moves closer.

David reaches for Susan's eyes. Just in time the educarer touches his hand and gently strokes both babies, softly saying, "David, you want to touch Susan's eyes, but eyes are delicate. We touch faces very gently."

Resources for Infant Educarer (RIE), founded in 1978, is a non-profit membership organization concerned with improving the care and education of infants. RIE offers parent-infant guidance classes,

Reprinted with permission of Zero to Three: National Center for Infants, Toddlers, and Families certification training for professionals, public workshops and conferences, and consultations to infant group care centers. These services all present the RIE approach, a humanistic-therapeutic way of working with infants based on my psychoanalytic training and work as a child therapist. To emphasize how educating and caring for an infant should be inseparable, I coined the words "educarer" and "educaring" to describe RIE's surprisingly simple and commonsensical philosophy, which differs so markedly from current trends.

We should educate while we care and care while we educate. Most people think of stimulating, exercising and teaching infants as important, glamorous activities. They think of diapering, feeding and bathing as unpleasant or mundane daily chores. RIE, however, suggests that caring activities are the optimal times for interaction, cooperation, intimacy and mutual enjoyment, providing social learning experiences which encourage full participation of the infant and her educarer. "Refueled" by such caring experiences, infants are ready to explore their environment with only minimal intervention by adults. A predictable balance of togetherness and separateness is achieved which benefits both infants and adults.

The RIE Philosophy: Observing the Infant Explorer

Giving the infant time, attention, trust and respect is the foundation of the RIE philosophy. Our goal is an authentic child—one who feels secure, autonomous, and competent. Our method, guided by respect for the infant's competence, is observation. RIE trusts the infant to be an initiator, an explorer and a self-learner. Because of this basic trust, we provide the infant with the minimal help she needs to overcome an impasse and allow the child to enjoy mastery of her own actions.

Educators are sensitive observers—available when direct help is needed, but not intrusive when the infant can solve her own problems. We provide an environment for the child that is physically safe, cognitively challenging and emotionally nurturing. There the child may freely explore and manipulate, fully involved in learning projects of her own design.

We allow infants to do what they are ready and willing to do. We reinforce their self-initiated activities by paying full attention, while being quietly available, and by appreciating and enjoying what the infants actually do. Occasional reflections such as "You touched the ball, and it rolled away" reassure the child of our full attention. Saying "It's hard to separate the two cups" shows our empathy. A joyful smile when the infant solves a problem conveys our pleasure in his success. As we value inner directedness in a child, we prefer gentle validations to instructions, to criticism, and even to praise.

Contrast with Other Approaches

This approach contrasts strongly with those used in most infant programs. In programs I have visited, children are taught, encouraged and expected to do what they are basically not ready to do. Too many infants are being propped up when they cannot yet maintain a well-balanced sitting position, or are given a toy which they have neither freely chosen nor can freely manipulate. Similarly, putting infants into devices such as infant seats, walkers, swings, or bouncers restricts them from moving freely. Such devices introduce positions or movement for which the infant is not yet ready.

RIE believes that a child who has always been allowed to move freely develops not only an agile body, but also good judgment about what he can and cannot do. Developing good body image, spatial relations and a sense of balance helps the child learn not only how to move, but also how to fall and how to recover. Children raised this way hardly ever have any serious accidents.*

---

* At the National Methodological Institute for Residential Nurseries, better known as Loczy, in Budapest, Hungary, more than 2,000 infants have been raised with the philosophy described here. In 37 years of raising infants from zero to three, they have had no serious accidents.

In contrast to the "experts," reinforced by the media, who urge parents to raise "superbabies," RIE emphasizes the benefits of infants' spending peaceful, uninterrupted time following their biological rhythms of falling asleep when sleepy and eating when hungry, rather than having to adjust too soon to external schedules and unrealistic expectations. We try to reassure parents that infants *do* do what they *can* do—and should not be expected to do what they are not ready for.

Parents in the RIE program learn how infant and family rhythms develop into predictable routines and how "separate time" and "together time" can be enjoyed. When infants are allowed uninterrupted play time between caregiving activities, parents can have their own time as well. Children who have learned to rely on being stimulated, manipulated and entertained by adults may lose their capacities to be absorbed in independent, exploratory activities. Their parents easily become slaves of the nagging child/tired parent syndrome they themselves helped unwittingly to create.

As parents and professional students learn to observe, they realize that being "busy" can keep one from intimacy, from really giving oneself, from paying attention. They began to see how many parents work too hard and try too hard—carrying babies around through sleepless nights, buying expensive toys, learning crib and teaching kits; teaching, programming, and following prescribed curricula and forgetting what is most important—that all those everyday, routine experiences, like feeding, dressing, bathing and diapering have the greatest effect on their baby. We remind parents of the cumulative effect diapering alone—which occurs some 7,000 times in an infant's life—can have on their child.

The following sample dialogue illustrates the interaction and learning opportunities in an everyday encounter.

Carer	Infant	Infant Learns:
Greets child "You seem to be having a good time with your rubber giraffe." *Tells and shows what she is going to do.* "But I want to pick you up and diaper you."	Pays Attention	To Anticipate *To Pay Attention*
Waits for Infant's Reaction "You're not quite ready so I'll wait a little. (One or two minutes later)	Responds to the Initiations of Carer (Positively or Negatively)	To Be Responsive to Each Other's Expectations
Asks for Cooperation or Follows Child's Lead "First we have to remove your overalls. You pull out your foot."	Cooperates and Participates	The Joy of Pleasing and Actively Participating
Encourages Mastery "You helped with this (touches foot) now pull out the other foot."	Achieves Mastery, Becomes Playful, Teasing, Doing the Opposite of What Is Asked	Infant Learns: The Joy of Mastery, Autonomy, Security Challenge
Enters the Game but Eventually gets Back to Task (*business*). "This (smiling) doesn't look like a foot, but more like a hand to me."	Enjoys the Process: Laughs	The Joy of Doing a Task Together

RIE Principles in Group Care

We believe that their own home is the natural habitat for the infant. Many infants, however, spend many hours, and sometimes their whole waking day, in group care. While RIE principles are applicable wherever infants are raised, their use is particularly important in the context of group infant care.

To be very special to the people who care for him or her is the right of each infant. This being special and being important is usually experienced within the child's own family. It gives the child a sense of self and a sense of belonging. Group care must work especially hard to impart this sense, since even with understanding staff, the child becomes one of many. It is therefore all the more important that during caregiving activities a special relationship develops between the infant and the carer, who would ideally be the same person over time. The idiosyncrasies, the unique style and tempo of each infant should be acknowledged and respected. The infant also learns to adapt to the characteristics of his special caregiver. This kind of relationship helps the child develop a sense of his own identify.

Group care can be beneficial when the environment and schedule are:

- set up to serve the child's needs
- predictable and consistent and
- allow the child to explore and interact with other infants.

These conditions can be met most easily in a small group of 4-6 babies or toddlers. Environment and scheduling combined with special relationships during caring may compensate for the loss of time spent at home.

Professional Certification Training

In RIE professional certification training classes, educators develop observational skills, become sensitive to each infant's needs and personal characteristics, and learn how to convey a feeling of specialness to an infant even though he must share carers.

The three phases of RIE training include comparison of infant development theories, observation of local infant environments and demonstration of the RIE approach in our parent-infant classes. Our own unique audio-visual library, including films of infants raised at the Loczy Institute, Hungary, and film, slide shows and videotapes made of our own programs, provide additional resources of our RIE interns.

Our students come from diverse disciplines, geographic areas and work settings. They are nurses, physical therapists, psychologists, early childhood educators, social workers, child care workers, family day care providers and administrators. They work with normal, at-risk and handicapped infants and their families.

RIE programs offer professional training,* parent-infant guidance classes and community education. Our work is both therapeutic and preventive. We believe that infancy is a crucial time to develop basic patterns of trusting, relating and learning. RIE supports wellness from the beginning of life.

··

Questions about Reading 1

1. When Magda used to train educators, she loved to watch one baby touch another. What did you think about that scene in the first paragraph. Would you allow one eight month old baby to touch another? Why or why not? Why do you think Magda allowed it?

---

* For professionals from outside of the Los Angeles area we offer a two-week RIE intensive training. Contact RIE, 1550 Murray Circle, Los Angeles, CA 90026. (213) 663-9610 or 663-5330.

2. Magda states that "most people think of stimulating, exercising and teaching infants as important, glamorous activities. They think of diapering, feeding and bathing as unpleasant or mundane daily chores." Is that true of you? Explain your answer in the space below.

3. Was there anything that particularly struck you about this article? Can you relate anything in it to your own life?

Chapter 2

Infant-Toddler Education

L ooking back at Chapter 2 in your text, think about how Lally seeks to define and describe the term curriculum. How does it relate to the information in Chapter 2? The concept of curriculum is difficult to explain when it relates to *infant-toddler* care and education rather than to education for older children. You can see how both Lally and the authors of your text work at making these ideas clear.

Reading 2

....

Curriculum and Lesson Planning: A Responsive Approach

J. Ronald Lally, Ed.D., August 1997

J. Ronald Lally, Ed.D., is director of WestEd's Center for Child and Family Studies, in Sausalito, California. He also directs the Program for Infant/Toddler Caregivers, a video-based training program. He is one of the founding members of Zero To Three.

In the United States of America we have related to infant and toddler development in a peculiar way. We have practiced curriculum extremes. One camp feels that all infants and toddlers need are safe environments and tender loving care and that intellectual activity is unnecessary, while the other believes that infants needed to be intellectually stimulated by adult-directed developmentally appropriate activities in order for them to grow cognitively. In many other nations this is not the approach taken toward infant learning. It is understood that tender loving care is necessary, but that intellectual development must be based on an understanding of each child's innate motivation and interest in learning. In these countries curriculum focuses not on one pole or the other but on how to create a climate that supports child-initiated learning. In Italy and Germany, for example, caregivers study the children in their care and keep detailed records of children's interests and skills so that they can facilitate children's learning. They are trained to search for how to use the children's natural interests and curiosity to lead to appropriate early lessons. A good portion of their lesson planning for infants involves training caregivers to understand each infant's and toddler's development and how to relate to it. It would serve us well if we learned from their approach.

American child care managers need to come to grips with the fact that much of what they are requiring of their caregivers with regard to lesson plans is inappropriate. Anticipating that the caregivers will need to adapt their actions to the momentary needs and interests of each child should be an essential part of any lesson plan. Lesson planning for infants, if done correctly, should first explore ways to help caregivers get in tune with each infant they serve and learn from the infant what he or she needs, thinks, and feels. Second, they should include strategies to broaden the caregiver's relationship with each individual child. Third, they should include a number of possible approaches for relating to a child's unique thoughts and feelings, meeting his or her needs, and matching interest with activity. All components of lesson planning must include adaptation of the plan and subsequent caregiver action to match the infant's response.

Another critical planning component is the context of learning. Much of what infants need is not the planning of specific lessons but a wise adult who can create a rich setting for learning. Learning environments and policies of care—the climate for learning—are more important to infant development than specific lessons. Research has shown us that much of what needs to happen with infants is not specific lessons but the preparation of their caregivers to capitalize on natural learning opportunities.

A Responsive Curriculum

For the past twelve years the *Program for Infant Toddler Caregivers* has developed video and print materials to assist center and family day-care providers implement high-quality infant and toddler care. We have developed strategies that help caregivers read and respond to the intellectual, social, and emotional messages of the infants in their care and have recommended policies that help programs focus on the importance of the relationships between the caregiver and child, and the caregiver and family, as the foundation of good care. Our materials and approach have been used to train many trainers throughout the country, who in turn have trained thousands of caregivers. It has recently come to our attention that help is needed in selecting curriculum and in developing lesson plans. It is imperative that activities, environments, and interaction styles are responsive to the needs of infants and toddlers, respect the competencies infants and toddlers bring to each interaction, and reflect the young child's need for relationship-based experiences.

From all we know about how infants best learn we have concluded that they must have a hand in the selection of what they learn. Our approach to curriculum therefore includes the infant as an active partner in the process of curriculum selection. In this way it is a curriculum that is responsive and respectful of what the infant brings to and wants from each experience. This type of curriculum is different from most. It needs to be well planned yet remain dynamic enough to move and flow with changing infant interests. It needs to anticipate developmental stages, but it also needs to allow for individual variations in learning style. It also must be broad enough in scope to respond to all developmental domains simultaneously. For example, just because you think you are teaching about object permanence it doesn't mean that is what the child is learning. He or she may be learning about their prescribed role in learning relationships.

In a responsive curriculum a good portion of lesson planning has to do with preparing caregivers and environments so that lessons can be learned. Implementation of a responsive curriculum involves training caregivers to understand and relate to infant and toddler development generally and also specifically. Much of lesson planning explores ways to help caregivers get in tune with each infant they serve and learn from the infant what he or she needs, thinks, and feels. When this is accomplished, often lessons being learned become quite obvious. Yet even "in tune" caregivers need to plan and re-plan how to form a relationship with and best meet each individual child's needs and relate to that child's unique thoughts and feelings. In a responsive curriculum often the most critical curriculum components are not lessons but the planning of settings that allow learning to take place. If the curriculum isn't planned so that environments, materials, group size, and management policies don't maximize the child's sense of security in care and in connection with the caregivers, promote a safe and interesting place to learn, and optimize connections with the child's family, very little positive learning will take place regardless of what lessons are planned.

Curriculum Planning: A Place to Begin

Because infants and toddlers have unique needs, their care must be constructed specifically to meet those needs. Good infant-toddler care is not babysitting and is not preschool. It is a special kind of care that looks like no other. For curriculum to be designed well and carried out appropriately, lesson plans, environments, routines, staffing, group size, relationships with families, and supervision and training must have as their starting point the following ten factors that differentiate infant-toddler care from the care of older children.

1. Infants and toddlers experience life more holistically than any other age group. Social, emotional, intellectual, language, and physical lessons are not separated by the infant. Adults who are most helpful to the young child interact in ways that understand that the child is learning from the whole experience, not just that part of the experience to which the adult gives attention.

2. Between birth and age three a child goes through three distinct developmental stages, and the type of care given needs to change as the stage changes and also takes into consideration transitions between stages.

3. The infant is dependent on close, caring, ongoing relationships as the source of positive, physical, social, emotional, and intellectual growth. Infants develop best when they are assured of having a trusted caregiver or caregivers who can read their cues and respond to their needs. Infant-toddlers care policy must be organized to ensure that these relationships exist and prosper. Policies that encourage and nurture these secure relationships are the backbone of quality care.

4. An infant or toddler learns most of how he or she thinks and feels by imitating and incorporating the behaviors of those around him or her. For this reason it is particularly important that caregivers be carefully selected and well trained.

5. Each infant is born curious and motivated to learn and actively participates in learning each day. Caregivers need specific training in infant learning to understand how to read and respond to infant behavior and to delight in the types of learning in which the infants are engaged. They also need training in how to construct environments and activities that keep motivation, experimentation, and curiosity alive and how to facilitate the infant learning process.

6. All children come into the world temperamentally different from each other, and because of these differences they need to be treated differently by their caregivers.

7. Parents and caregivers of infants and toddlers often experience a heightened sense of emotionality related to the care of the infants and toddlers. Strategies for dealing with conflicts that can emerge from this "protective urge" must be considered as part of care.

8. Much of the first two years of life are spent in the creation of a child's first "sense of self" or the building of a first identity. Because this is such a crucial part of children's makeup—how they first see themselves, how they think they should function, how they expect others to function in relation to them—early care must ensure that in addition to carefully selected and trained caregivers, links with family, home culture, and home language are a central part of program policy. If care becomes a substitute for, rather than a support of, family, children will often incorporate a less-than-positive sense of who they are and where they come from because of their infant care experience.

9. The development of language is particularly crucial during the infant-toddler period. Good care provides many opportunities for infants to engage in meaningful and context-based dialogue with their caregivers and to have the child's communications acknowledged and encouraged.

10. Infants and toddlers are strongly influenced by the environments and routines they are subjected to each day. This is particularly true for very young infants who cannot physically move themselves from a noxious to a more pleasant environment. Physical environment, group size, daily schedules, lesson plans, and the conduct of routines must foster the establishment of small inti-

mate groups in which relationships with trusted caregivers can be established and have a chance to grow and become the base for social, emotional, and intellectual learning in a safe and interesting environment.

....

Questions about Reading 2

1. Lally defines curriculum *extremes* as either 1. "all infants and toddlers need are safe environments and tender loving care." Or 2. "infants need to be intellectually stimulated by adult-directed developmentally appropriate activities." What do you think?

2. Lally uses the term "lesson" in his article. What do you think he means?

3. He also states, "American child care managers need to come to grips with the fact that much of what they are requiring of their caregivers with regard to lesson plans is inappropriate." Have you had experience writing lesson plans for infants and toddlers? If yes, do you agree or disagree with his statement? Why?

4. What do you think he means when he says, "the infant should be 'an active partner' in the process of curriculum selection"?

Chapter 3

Caregiving as Curriculum

After reading chapter 3 in your text, you may come to the conclusion that working with infants and toddlers is different from working with, say, four year olds. Just because caregivers are good at working with preschool children, doesn't mean they can automatically take what they know and apply it to infants. In this article, Kovach and Da Ros consider some of the differences between the two age groups. This article is compatible with the philosophy of Magda Gerber, which, along with Emmi Pikler's approach, is the core of *Infants, Toddlers, and Caregivers*. As you read this article, notice the number of examples and illustrations of the 10 principles in action. We learn best when we can see examples, both in real life, and by reading about them.

Reading 3

....

Respectful, Individual, and Responsive Caregiving for Infants

The Key to Successful Care in Group Settings

Beverly A. Kovach and Denise A. Da Ros

Beverly A. Covach, M.N., founder of a private Montessori school in Charleston, South Carolina, for infants through six years, is a family therapist, Montessori infant-toddler specialist, and RIE (Resources for Infant Educators) fellow of Magda Gerber. Her workshops and publications focus on respectful interactions with infants and toddlers that support self-confidence.

Denise A. Da Ros, Ph.D., is an assistant professor of early childhood education at Youngstown State University in Ohio. She has had extensive experience directing early childhood programs.

Group care often fails to meet the needs of babies and frequently compromises healthy infant development. Alarmingly, the landmark Cost, Quality, and Child Outcomes study (1995) found that most infant group care settings probably harm children's development and learning. Group care also is costly and in short supply.

Expert practice, theory, and research on what constitutes best practice in child care and what fosters optimal physical, cognitive, and socioemotional development of infants have been slow to transform everyday caregiving practice (Pikler 1978), often because caregivers have insufficient training opportunities.

Studies on intimacy and self-efficiency (for example, Curry & Johnson 1990) show that to support an infant's sense of well-being and personal power, it is crucial for her to get her need met as soon as she indicates a need (Bell & Ainsworth 1972). Caregivers must be attuned and sensitive to the individual infant. This sensitive—that is, responsive—caregiving is the most important factor in determining the quality of infant care (Lozoff et al. 1977).

Leavitt says responsive caregiving "goes beyond physical caretaking. It includes a sense of personal and emotional involvement that is mutual" (1994, 70). Respectful and responsive caregiving is the core of fostering and maintaining trust between the infant and caregiver.

Good caregivers provide interactions that fully support individual care and include the babies themselves in the caregiving and decisionmaking process (Bower 1976; Honig 1981). Babies tend to thrive when they are consistently included in their own care (Beckwith 1971). This approach affords the baby continuity of care, sensitive, and attuned interactions, and responsive care.

To provide a more complete picture of what sensitive and competent infant care is, we offer the following seven principles. We also give inappropriate and appropriate caregiving situations to highlight each principle.

Inappropriate: A six- and a four-month-old infant sit next to each other in musical mechanical swings with the tunes clashing. As the caregiver feeds a three-month-old, she vigorously rocks her chair with one foot and with the other taps a bouncer that holds a crying baby. "Ssshhh," she keeps repeating.

Appropriate: Soft music plays. Two babies are on separate blankets, each with a few objects within easy reach. Sometimes the infants grasp the toys; sometimes they gaze out the low, nearby window. The caregiver, who is feeding Matthew on her lap, smiles at the babies and returns her attention to Matthew.

Rationale: Sensitive caregiving includes creating a calm and peaceful environment for infants while they are being fed or diapered. The caregiver needs to be aware of how unhurried focused care—her "fully there time" (Gerber 1979)—influences physical care times. Her ability to stay focused on an individual infant is in part reliant on her trust that the other babies are content to play quietly once their physical needs have been met.

Inappropriate: Mary notices a smelly diaper. She asks her companion caregiver, "Did you change Chelsea before putting her down?" When her coworker responds no, Mary goes to the crib, picks up Chelsea, and wordlessly proceeds to change her diaper. "Who else in the room needs to be changed?' she asks as she lays Chelsea down and walks away.

Appropriate: When Mary notices an odor, she stops at the crib and says, "Chelsea, I need to check your diaper." She extends her hands and waits for the baby's response before picking her up. At the changing table, she tells Chelsea exactly what she is going to do before she does it, and she gives her enough time to respond to her caregiving. Before putting Chelsea down, Mary again tells her what she is going to do.

Rationale: Caregivers often talk *about* infants rather than *to* infants. When adults ignore an infant during caregiving times, the message given is that the baby does not rate personal and undivided attention. When staff are better trained and talk with the infants, the children also tend to do better in language development (Tizard et al. 1972).

Inappropriate: Five babies, ranging in age from five months to a year old, are at a table, their feet dangling in midair. Three slumped to the side and the other two sit upright. Two are crying. None of the babies can reach her bowl or spoon. A caregiver methodically pushes a spoon into the mouth of the first baby, then the second, and so on.

Appropriate: Nine-month-old Emily is sitting at a weaning table; her chair sized so she can get up and down by herself and her feet touch the floor. In front of her is a bowl and two spoons. The caregiver, who sits opposite Emily, lets the baby attempt to feed herself, occasionally giving her a bit with a spoon. She uses normal language in telling Emily what she is doing before she does it, and she waits and observes the baby's reaction before acting.

Rationale: Many adults operate on the assumption that infants are helpless. This assumption motivates caregivers to put or place infants in positions that they are not ready for or are not able to support by themselves. Self-induced, independent movements create favorable, emotional, and intellectual development (Pikler 1969). Magda Gerber, renowned infant specialist, advises caregivers, "Allow infants to do what it is they are ready and willing to do. . . . Self-initiated activities need to be reinforced by being quietly available and enjoying what the infants actually do" (1984, 2).

Inappropriate: A caregiver sits on the floor to feed James, who is confined in a bouncer. Sulee, curious, crawls over. After repeated attempts to ignore the intruding child, the frustrated caregiver stops feeding, picks up Sulee, puts her in another part of the room, and returns to the task of feeding James.

Appropriate: James, a five-month-old, is being held while being bottle fed. The caregiver's actions are unhurried, and her attention is focused on James. Because the feeding area is separate from the exploratory play area, nothing interrupts her time with James.

Rationale: Infants deserve uninterrupted, individual caregiving. Their well-being requires caregivers to invest in quality time while providing physical care.

Inappropriate: Eight-month-old Kisha, who has crawled under a rocking chair, begins to cry. Her caregiver, noting her distress, bends down and lifts her up, saying, "You're all right. You're all right."

Appropriate: Kisha crawls under a child's table and begins to cry. Her caregiver drops to her hands and knees and calmly talks to Kisha, encouraging her to crawl out. She waits for the baby's reaction. Kisha, who appears afraid to move forward with her head, cries louder. The caregiver slowly reaches forward and gently places her hand on Kisha's head, while telling the baby what she is doing with her. By providing just enough help to move out from under the table, the caregiver is reinforcing the infant's involvement in helping to solve this problem.

Rationale: As adults, we do not like to see infants struggle. But by not allowing babies to use their natural competencies, we teach them to become victims. Caregivers need to provide just enough help for the baby to problem-solve his own dilemma (Honig 1981). The baby then becomes a valued participant in his own care and develops positive self-esteem.

Inappropriate: A caregiver, looking over the daily activity sheet, notes that Reed is supposed to have her bottle by 4 o'clock. But Reed is still sleeping, and it's 4:05 now. Knowing that Reed's mom will be coming at 4:30, the caregiver wakes up the infant, hurriedly changes her diaper, and begins to feed her a bottle.

Appropriate: The caregiver goes over to Reed, who is resting peacefully, and she makes a mental note to check the sleeping infant in 15 to 20 minutes. She records her observations on Reed's daily activity sheet.

Rationale: A caregiver is better able to meet a baby's individual needs if she observes the behaviors and responses of the child and includes these in the baby's care. Caregivers also may have to help parents understand that a baby's individual schedule is what is best for her.

Inappropriate: Two-month-old Brent begins to cry. The caregiver goes to the crib and puts a pacifier in his mouth.

Appropriate: The caregiver goes to Brent and says softly. "I hear you, but I don't know why you are crying. Let me pick you up and see about your diaper and check when you had your last feeding."

Rationale: Because it is hard for adults to listen to a baby cry, our immediate response is to stop the crying. But crying is a form of infant communication, and our role as caregivers is to try to understand what the baby is communicating. Is he hungry, tired, wet, thirsty, or startled? By reacting instead of interacting, we exclude the baby from the process of his care.

* * *

Society in general does not appreciate babies as separate and valued persons. Indeed, children's stature correlates with teacher status; the younger the children he teaches, the lower the teacher's wages, education, and prestige. Because a lack of individualized care can cause serious damage to the psychosocial well-being of the young, caregivers must be nurturing and give responsive infant care (Kagan, Kearsley, & Zelazo 1976).

We need to focus on the importance of learning in the first year of life. Although difficult, individualized care can be provided in group settings. Care needs to be based on a consistent philosophy that includes the infant as an active participant.

Providing sensitive caregiving to infants in group care requires administrators who understand and support infant needs; a program that is affordable and accessible to families; a staff-parent partnership on behalf of the baby; and most important, a staff that is well trained. According to the National Day Care Study, staff training is what determines the quality of the program (Ruopp et al. 1979). There is a critical need and an emerging national interest to provide and procure specialized training for caregivers of children under three.

Educarers (Gerber 1979) need to work with others to revamp societal norms so that responsive and respectful caregiving includes the infant while he or she is in group care. Resources must be allocated to initiate and carry out a plan of care that speaks to the individual needs of infant autonomy while in group care. Individualizing infant care and incorporating respectful and responsive caregiving allow each infant to maintain her own preferences and sense of self. What better way of demonstrating this than to give undivided attention during infant caregiving?

References

Beckwith, L. 1971. Relationships between attritubes of mothers and their infants' IQ scores. *Child Development* 42 (4): 1083–97.

Bell, S., & M.D.S. Ainsworth. 1972. Infant crying and maternal responsiveness. *Child Development* 43: 1171–90.

Bower, T.G.R. 1976. *Development in infancy.* San Francisco: W.H. Freeman.

Child Care Action Campaign. 1988. Child care: The bottom line. *Child Care ActionNews* 5 (5): 1.

Cost, Quality, & Outcomes Study Team. 1995. Cost, quality, and child outcomes in child care centers: Key findings and recommendations. *Young Children* 50 (4): 40–44.

Curry, N.E., & C.N. Johnson. 1990. *Beyond Self-Esteem: Developing a genuine sense of human value.* Research Monograph of the National Association of Young Children. vol. 4. Washington, DC: NAEYC.

Gerber, M.A., ed. 1979. *Resources for infant educarers.* Los Angeles: Resources for Infant Educarers.

Gerber, M.A. 1984. Caring for infants with respect: The RIE approach. *Zero to Three* 4 (3): 1–3.

Honig, A. 1981. Recent infant research. In *Infants and their social environments,* eds. B. Weissbourd & J. Musick, 5–46. Washington, DC: NAEYC.

Kagan, J., R.B. Kearsley, & P. Zelazo, 1976. The effects of infant day care on psychological development. *ERIC Newsletter* 10 (2).

Leavitt, R.L. 1994. *Power and emotion in infant-toddler day care.* Albany: State University of New York Press.

Lozoff, B., G. Brillenham, M.A. Trause, J.H. Kennell, & M.H. Klaus. 1977. The mother-newborn relationship: Limits of adaptability. *Journal of Pediatrics* 91 (July).

Pikler, E. 1969. *Data on gross-motor development of the infant.* Budapest. Hungary: Publishing House of the Hungarian Academy of Science.

Pikler, E. 1978. The competence of the infant. *Acte Paediatrica Academiae Scientiarum Hungaricae* 20: 185–92.

Ruopp, R. J. Travers, F. Glantz, & C. Coelen. 1979. *Children at the center, final report of the National Day Care Study, Vol 1.* Washington, DC: Office of Human Development, U.S. Department of Health, Education, and Welfare.

Tizard, B., O. Cooperman, A. Joseph, & J. Tizard. 1972. Environmental effects on language development: A study of young children in long-stay residential nurseries. *Child Development* 4: 337–58.

For Further Reading

Balaban. N. 1992. The role of the child care professional in caring for infant, toddler, and their families. *Young Children* 47 (5): 66–71.

Gonzalez-Mena, J., & D. Eyer. 1995. *Infants, toddlers, and caregivers.* 4th ed. Mountain View, CA: Mayfield.

Honig, A. 1989. Quality infant-toddler caregiving: Are there magic recipes? *Young Children* 44 (4): 4–10.

Honig, A. 1993. Mental health for babies: What do theory and research teach us? *Young Children* 48 (3): 69–76.

Lally, R.J. 1995. The impact of child care policies and practices on infant-toddler identity formation. *Young Children* 51 (1): 59–67.

Weissbourd, B., & J. Musick, eds. 1981. *Infants and their social environments.* Washington: NAEYC.

Questions about Reading 3

1. Think about what you know or imagine about four-year-olds. How are the examples and illustrations in this article different from what they would be if the children were older? Write three differences below.

2. Honoring diversity is important. Pick two examples of inappropriate situations that don't seem inappropriate to you. Give your perspective on those situations and explain how a family might feel if their practice was labeled inappropriate by the staff or provider.

3. How can caregivers honor diversity, honor a particular philosophy, and also honor their own perspective?

Chapter 4

Play as Curriculum

Chapter 4 of your text focuses on play, an important part of the infant-toddler curriculum. Part of that chapter relates directly to what Anna Tardos had to say at a conference in Los Angeles[1] about how caregivers facilitate play at Loczy, the Pikler Institute in Budapest.

Reading 4

....

Facilitating the Play of Children at Loczy

Anna Tardos

Anna Tardos is child psychologist and the daughter of Emmi Pikler. She is also the director of the Pikler Institute in Budapest, which is nicknamed Loczy.

Playing in the usual sense is considered as starting at an age when the child is able to have, at the same time, two levels of awareness. While being aware of reality, he or she is also aware of the fantasy aspect of the play situation. But I am going to talk about play in a broader sense. When I refer to play, I mean a chance for uninhibited free activity, in most cases using an object to play with.

The starting point of our view is that play is simply the activity of children. Researchers have learned how an infant proceeds from one stage to another in her play development by observing children themselves. In no way do we see our task to teach children how to play or stimulate them to play. We are learning from the children how to play, rather than the children learning from us.

Our basic premise in facilitating children's play is that our help must always be indirect. We offer possibilities; the child makes the choice. For examples, it is our task to provide toys, but we never put any toy into the infant's hand.

In what way then do we promote or encourage play? First, we organize a peaceful, quiet environment. Contrary to general opinion found in the literature that infants should be inundated with stimuli, our opinion is that the young infant must be protected from too much stimuli. For example, for this reason we do not put young babies in the play pen for the first two-and-a-half to three months. We do not put any toys, especially the noisy ones, in his crib, neither during the first months nor later. We talk and move quietly in the room or outdoors, on the terrace and even in the yard, not only when the children are asleep, but also when they are awake and playing. We ask, for example, observers to close the door quietly when leaving.

---

[1] (Excerpt from a Lecture given at "More than Play" Conference, June 29, 1985, Los Angeles, California)

Secondly, we provide sufficient space for infants in which to move freely. Movement is one of the basic needs of infants. If you look at an infant from a distance, you can determine whether he or she is asleep or awake by seeing his body moving or being quiet. In our experience, infants' play activities are enhanced when they are not restricted from gross motor activities, such as changing position and changing places.

Space allocated for the play area is always somewhat larger than infants can use. For example, the infant who is just turning himself over is given space large enough for rolling. A rolling child is given space large enough for crawling or creeping.

Thirdly, the infant's play territory is fenced-in and safe from real dangers. Boundaries make it possible for the infant to become acquainted with each corner of his territory. He or she can repeatedly go to the same corner and find the same characteristic of the play area. This gives him the feeling of familiarity. If the space is too large, it is difficult for the infant to get acquainted with. That is our opinion.

A fenced-in area makes it possible to keep danger out. I want to mention, however, that we do not consider all unpleasant experiences in the course of play dangerous. Perhaps you would like me to tell you an example. If a child hits his head on the hard wooden floor, this is not really dangerous; rather this is going to be a useful experience, and will teach the child to be more careful. But unexpected real accidents can hurt the infant's desire for autonomous activity. He may lose confidence in moving and activity. For example, if the chair he is holding onto tips over and hits the child, this is a real danger.

Real danger causes the adult in charge to interfere in the child's action, and hampers the infant's activity. In this case the adult must continually say, "Do not do this, do not touch that," and this will hamper and restrict the child, disturbing movement and activity.

The fourth important element in facilitating the play of infants is the choice of objects. We find that the opportunities for activity offered by the objects are more important than the adult appeal of the object. Thus, few of the toys we give to infants emit sound, especially not the first toys. In our opinion, the more simple the toy, the more suitable for infants' use. Sparkling, glittering and sound-producing toys elicit surprise, but do not promote a variety of activities. Such toys reduce the infant's sensitivity threshold, and the infant then needs ever-more sophisticated toys to induce a response. This would be similar to a drug-induced effect.

In contrast to this would be a colored cotton scarf. It introduces no sound, it is not sparkling, it is not glittery, but becomes engrossing through its capacity to produce many variants of movement, and it is also safe.

When we offer the child a toy, it is important that it should provide opportunities for play consistent with the child's current and future capacity for activity. For example, we offer many hollow objects even before the child is ready for the activity of putting something inside. I wish to emphasize that we always present that which is attainable, and it is always the child who decides which toy to play with and what the play will be. For example, he or she may want to just swat the hollow objects.

These are only some small examples of our approach to facilitating the play of young children.

. . . .

Questions about Reading 4

1. You may have had some reactions and feelings as you read this excerpt from Anna Tardos's speech. If you did, what was it specifically that you were reacting to? What were your feelings? Do you have some ideas about why you had those reactions?

2. Why do you think adults tend to buy glittery toys that make noises and surprise infants? Do you agree with Anna that simple toys are better?

3. Novelty and surprise are valued by many in the United States. Do you think the simple toys and lack of surprises are a cultural difference between Americans of the dominant culture and Hungarians?

Chapter 5

Attachment

C hapter 5 of your text focuses on attachment as an important requirement for a sense of trust, which greatly contributes to the kind of security that makes for a healthy personality. Having a primary caregiver system helps insure that each infant has a relationship with a caregiver outside his or her family, though of course, family members still have the most influential relationships with the child. This article tells how to set up such a system and gives clear details about how to address the obstacles that can get in the way of its implementation.

Reading 5

A Primary Caregiving System for Infants and Toddlers: Best for Everyone Involved

Jennifer L. Bernhardt

Jennifer L. Bernhardt has worked as an infant/toddler caregiver, administrator, and consultant who has helped implement the primary caregiving model in programs serving children birth to three. She is an infant massage instructor and at the time of the article she was a writer and an adult educator.

The term *primary caregiver* has long been used in research to describe the most significant adult person in a child's life, usually the mother. As the care of infants and toddlers outside the home has increased over the last three decades, the term *primary caregiving* has evolved to describe a model or system of caring for children in groups.

Although primary caregiving has caught on across the country—and experts on quality care issues often imply a primary caregiving system or even mention it by name in their writing—many caregivers working in infant and toddler care settings don't understand what it is, why it is done, or how to make it work. Or worse, staff mistakenly believe they are working under the primary caregiving model when they are not. A thorough understanding of primary caregiving is important for all staff working directly or indirectly with young children in groups.

regiving model, each caregiver or teacher within a larger group is assigned primary
ecific group of children. For example, in an infant-care room with a ratio of three to
bies, each caregiver is responsible for the care of the same three children every day.
he caregiver cares exclusively for the same three children; rather, that she has princi-
the few children in her direct care.

g caregivers is absolutely essential for the system to run smoothly and effectively. This
coverage approach in which caregivers collectively care for all children by assigning
tasks—one caregiver changes all diapers in the morning, another feeds all the children breakfast, and so on.

Advantages of Primary Caregiving

The main advantage of primary caregiving is the bond that forms between the child and adult through constant daily interactions. According to Eriksonian theory, the first component of a healthy personality is a sense of trust, the foundations of which develop during the first 18 months of a child's life. This sense of trusting the world is key to a child's healthy psychological development (Erikson 1963). Of course, the parent-child relationship is far and away the most influential relationship a young child has, but his relationship with his full-time child care provider is very important too.

John Bowlby's (1969) attachment theory tells us that infants internalize aspects of their self/caregiver relationships. The models they build are unconscious, yet they serve as models for other close relationships later (Honig 1993). If the relationship the child care provider builds with the young child affects how he approaches all future relationships, the provider has a responsibility to work on developing the most trustful and pleasurable relationship she can.

The child and adult learn each other's rhythms and responses through their daily interactions, and each becomes skilled at anticipating the actions of the other. Knowing what to expect contributes to the child's feeling of security. Knowing how to elicit certain responses from a caring adult gives her a sense of control over her world. These factors all help a child begin to feel a strong sense of self-worth and value.

A trusted caregiver serves as a home base for her children. An infant or toddler who is confident that her caregiver is close by and available is willing to move out and explore the world on her own. This may simply mean that a child feels safe enough to crawl a few feet away to examine a new toy because she knows she will be able to get help from her special adult if she needs it. Very young children who do not have a special, trusted caregiver may become angry or excessively clingy. But children who feel close to a special adult learn that it is safe to move away, explore for a while, then come back to "refuel," as Mahler, Pine, and Bergman (1975, 2) call it.

A sensitive caregiver observes her children's interactions and demonstrates positive interactions with others. She is aware that a young child identifies with her and with her behaviors and patterns his own behaviors after hers. The caregiver knows her children well enough to know when to intervene in a difficult situation between two or more of them. She helps her individual children learn to negotiate and cooperate with one another, as much as their developmental levels allow, and helps them learn to be sensitive to others' needs.

Forging emotional bonds

Once an infant has developed object permanence (the realization that even when something is out of reach, it still exists), he will often cry in protest when his parent leaves him in the morning. Separation can be sad and painful for both child and parent. Having a significant other there to hold him and get him involved in something that interests him eases the transition from home to group care and makes separation less traumatic and often as easy as a kiss good-bye when Mom or Dad leaves. Even for a child who always has a hard time with separations, the emotional support the primary caregiver provides is priceless.

What about a child who hasn't formed a strong emotional bond with a parent or other family member? The caregiver may be the only person the child can fully trust and depend on. This emotional bond becomes vital for the child's well-being and serves as a protective factor in his development (Wittmer 1995). It is all the more important for any child at risk of being overwhelmed by stress factors—and especially children who are separated from their parents on a regular basis—to be cared for by one loving adult.

In a primary-care group in which a child shares a primary caregiver with two or three other children, the child often forms a strong bond not just with the primary caregiver but with the other children in the group as well. Such bonds mimic sibling bonds and may be especially rewarding for children who do not have siblings at home. Two babies in my primary care, for example, formed a very strong bond early on. The girls were rarely more than a few feet from each other and often fell into the same daily pattern of eating and napping. For a time I even held both—one in my arm, the other in my lap—as they drank their morning bottles. The girls moved together through the center, supporting each other and remaining fast friends. The child–child bond is an especially important one in a program in which children do not have the same primary caregiver for the first three years of their lives—which, unfortunately, seems to be the norm in many group-care settings.

Benefits are not only for the child

The primary caregiving system does not benefit only the children; it frequently has a positive effect on the caregiver's sense of value.

Employees whose supervisors help them develop skills and gradually gain control over their work environment are happier and more productive. The staff person in a primary caregiving setting is responsible for the daily care of her children. She plans for, observes, and evaluates them on an ongoing basis, changing routines or the environment as they grow. The caregiver develops a sense of pride and achievement, as well as a sense of importance to the group as a whole. The caregiver's added responsibilities and chances to work more closely with her supervisor or mentor that may arise from primary caregiving are on-the-job training for more advanced teaching positions.

I have seen many center directors struggle to increase morale and find ways to enhance staff feelings of pride and ownership in the group. I have also noticed that implementing the primary caregiving model increases staff morale almost immediately!

Maybe even more important to the caregiver than a sense of control in the workplace is the daily reward of seeing the positive effect she has on the lives of her primary children. She sees them grow physically, emotionally, intellectually, and socially and knows she is playing a very important role in their development. The ultimate reward is that many of the children's smiles are meant only for her!

Parents reap rewards too

Parents also reap the rewards of a trusting relationship with the caregiver. Having one adult primarily responsible for their child all day means that the parents have one primary contact with whom to communicate and share information.

Imagine a parent who calls the center during his lunch break to find out how his daughter's morning has been. A caregiver answers the phone but knows only that his daughter had a bowel movement around 9:00 A.M. That staff member asks another caregiver nearby, but she knows only that his daughter finished her morning bottle and that a third caregiver played with her outside for a while around 10:30. However, the third caregiver is on her lunch break and won't return until the parent is in an afternoon meeting. Sadly, this is a common scenario for parents whose children are in a setting that follows a task-assignment approach.

In the primary caregiving model, parents know whom to ask for when they call the center. They also know the caregiver's work schedule, so they can call before or after her breaks. The caregiver in turn knows the parents well, having formed a bond with them as well as with their child. Together, they share information about the child's development and needs and work to make positive decisions about the child's care.

Best of all, the parents feel comfortable leaving their child in care. When I mentioned that the caregiver eases the separation anxiety that often arises during drop-off times, I meant anxiety for the parent too! Parents who are anxious and uneasy send out nonverbal—and sometimes verbal—cues to children. Even a very young infant can sense a parent's body stiffening or other physical tension in response to arriving at the care site. If a child—even a very young infant—repeatedly picks up negative cues from a parent, she will begin to feel that this is not a safe place. On the other hand, a confident, happy parent gives the child the message that her care is good and safe, adding to the child's sense of comfort and security.

A parent who develops a relationship with the primary caregiver also is more likely to share important information about the child's home life. Without the single direct contact that primary caregiving provides, the parent may not want to share such personal information for the whole staff to know—and of course there must also be confidentiality! But with one significant adult to share information with, the parent may give information or suggestions that help the caregiver understand and more appropriately respond to and nurture the child.

In turn, a primary caregiver who has a strong bond with her families can advocate for needed changes or suggest new direction for growth in staff meetings, which high-quality centers hold every week or two with caregivers and administrators. As advocate the child care professional has a wonderful opportunity to create centerwide change that can improve the relationship between the center and all the families it serves.

Many possibilities arise just by building up trust in this triad of relationships!

Overcoming Obstacles

Although a child care setting is ideally limited to six children, with a ratio of three children to one adult, this is not always a reality in group care. In one of my first group-care experiences, I worked in a center that served up to 23 infants and toddlers in one large space. This was far from ideal. There were too many people "living" in this one area, and it often became overstimulating, even for me. The administration eventually limited the number of children to sixteen, with a 4:1 child-to-caregiver ratio, but it was still a difficult situation. Primary caregiving ameliorates the effects of such a large group setting.

If staff members find themselves in such undesirable circumstances, the most important thing to do is lobby for fewer sets of infants or toddlers and caregivers per room. However, giving each child a primary caregiver can help everyone. Even in a room of six children and two caregivers, all still benefit from primary caregiving. The children will most likely form bonds with both caregivers in the small group, but routine consistency and knowing what to expect from one special adult are still essential to the child's development of positive self-esteem.

In many group settings, a senior teacher or caregiver is the leader and supervisor of the other staff in the room. Primary caregiving does not interrupt this staffing hierarchy. The senior teacher can be a primary caregiver if group numbers and ratios require it. When staff members' professional preparation has not been optimal, the senior teacher should be someone who can effectively help others develop caregiving insights and skills.

Some settings have one more adult than is needed to meet the ratio in the group. If this extra adult is an assistant or intern, the senior teacher should remain a primary caregiver and the extra staff person serve as a helper to all staff, interacting with all of the children. However, if all the adults are qualified and can effectively carry out the roles of a primary caregiver, then all staff except the senior teacher should be primary caregivers, leaving the senior teacher to help, supervise, and have more flexibility to leave the care room if necessary.

In any case, one extra adult serves an important role in the group-care setting. She helps the other staff when more children need immediate attention than there are primary caregivers and is the familiar person who fills in the primary caregiving role during a staff person's absence. Prompt responsiveness to needy babies and one- and two-year-olds is a hallmark of good care.

It should be the policy in any child care setting to limit the total number of adults who care for children under three years old. If there are no extra staff or floaters in the center with whom the children can become familiar, administrators should strive to use the same few substitutes, so the children recognize them and the substitutes get to know and understand the way the center works. It is also important to stagger staff working hours so all familiar people don't vanish at a certain hour when a new shift comes in.

Getting the Kinks Out

Some benefits to primary caregiving are not realized until the mechanics of the system work smoothly. It takes work to change to a primary caregiving system. Making it work effectively takes dedication and the belief that the change is for the best.

I've gone through this change with several centers and have found that it takes much practice and lots of communication between all parties involved to work out the kinks. But once the staff works under the primary caregiving model, it seems to become second nature. It is natural for adults who love children to want to bond with and provide quality care for them.

To start, the senior teacher or administrator assigns children to primary caregivers. In a setting in which all the adults have cared for the children, she first assigns children to the adults they have already formed a bond with. If a child has not bonded with any particular adult or has bonded with more than one adult, it makes sense to compare children's and caregiver's schedules and match them as closely as possible to maximize the time each child spends in the care of one special adult. (I have noticed that the natural bonds that form before primary caregiving is implemented often are between adults and children who have similar schedules.)

It also makes sense to match a caregiver with a family according to any special situations. If a caregiver previously formed a special bond with a child's older sibling and came to know the family well, it's usually wise to match the younger child with this caregiver. If a family is from the same culture or speaks the same language as a particular caregiver, the family may feel more comfortable with her. The senior teacher or administrator also should consider other unique circumstances.

An established program sometimes has no choice in the pairing, as one caregiver will have an opening and the newest child will fill it. Only in extremely problematic situations should a child switch from one caregiver to another in the same room once he has established a primary relationship. Ideally, every child should stay with the same caregiver through the age of three. In any case, children should be moved from caregiver to caregiver as infrequently as possible. Frequent changes are traumatic and defeat some of the advantages of the primary caregiving model.

Knowing Who's Responsible

Once children are assigned, each staff person should have a good understanding of her daily duties and responsibilities. These include, but aren't limited to, greeting each of her primary care children, easing transitions to and from the group setting as her work schedule allows, preparing food (being aware of any special diets or food allergies) and feeding the children, checking and changing diapers, putting children down for naps, supervising them at all times, and providing a loving atmosphere throughout the day.

The caregiver also is responsible for documenting these activities in a written report that goes home with each child's parent at the end of the day. In addition, she talks with the children's parents at least once during each day.

The primary caregiver also observes and documents the children's growth and development, plans appropriate individual and group activities, and works with the other staff and supervisors to add to or make changes in the environment to match children's developmental needs.

As stated before, primary caregiving does not mean that one person cares exclusively for an infant or toddler; there has to be teaming (Lally, Torres, & Phelps 1994). Each staff person must remain flexible and committed to quality care for every child in the program. A caregiver may be assigned to three children, but she must interact with others in the group. The primary caregiving relationship should be viewed as primary—not exclusive. This helps create other relationships that the infant can fall back on when the primary caregiver is unavailable (Lally 1995).

Staff members also must realize what a tremendous help they can be to one another. For example, Meesha, whose three children all arrive within 15 minutes of each other, wants to individually greet each child and parent, but her first arrival will be ready for his bottle very soon. Paulina, a second caregiver, is nearby and two of her children are sleeping. She helps Meesha by warming the bottle and holding one of the children whose parents have already gone. By pitching in and helping each other, everyone's needs are met and the children benefit.

When staff need immediate assistance and there is no time to ask questions, they should consult other staff members, when possible, before presuming to help out with their children. Crucial information may have been passed by the parents to their child's primary caregiver. For example, consider Jeanne. who is holding and calming Nancy, a six-month-old who is cutting two new teeth. Another of Jeanne's assigned children, Dale, is ready for breakfast. Sharon, an unoccupied staff member, decides to help Jeanne by preparing Dale's food. She goes to his cubby, gets two baby-food containers, heats them, and begins to feed Dale. Sharon means to help, but she didn't talk to Jeanne to find out that Dale's parents mentioned that they had left yesterday's that they had left yesterday's food containers in his cubby and the new ones were in his diaper bag. Sharon should have consulted Jeanne before helping out.

Doing the Dirty Work

Very few of even the most dedicated child care professionals want to change dirty diapers! A problem that often creeps up in primary-care settings is that a child stays in a dirty diaper until his own caregiver is available to change it because another caregiver states that "He's not my child!" A primary caregiver should routinely change her own children's diapers, but no child should be left unchanged when any adult is available to change him. Teamwork not only is a necessity but also a hallmark of a professional child care provider.

To ensure consistent care during staff breaks, caregivers may want to "partner up." Each makes sure that the other's children are cared for and that all interactions are recorded on the child's daily sheet. This partnering works even if a substitute is responsible for the children. It helps the substitute and provides a backup system to ensure that all the children's routines are documented.

Any time a staff member other than a child's primary caregiver performs a routine-care task with a child, she should record the appropriate information on the child's sheet. Next to the information she should place her initials so that staff and parents know whom to contact if any questions arise.

Every center has its own issues to work through. For this reason, centers should hold frequent staff meetings to discuss these situations and work out solutions.

A Combination of Care

With very young children spending increasing amounts of time in care settings away from their parents, a caregiver must provide experiences and an environment that promote trust, security, and positive self-esteem. Primary caregiving is one way to do this. The many benefits of this system can ameliorate the effects of less-than-perfect care situations.

To provide maximum high-quality care, other policies should be used in conjunction with a primary care-giving system, such as limited group sizes and low staff-child ratios. In addition, child care staff and administrators should do everything possible to allow a child to stay in the care of the same primary caregiver for the longest time possible—ideally, for the first three years. Only by implementing such policies can we begin to ensure that our youngest children grow up in an environment in which they feel safe and feel that they can trust the world.

....

Questions about Reading 5

1. How do you feel about having primary caregivers in an infant center? What are your thoughts on the subject?

2. Do you remember being attached as a child to someone outside the family? If yes, does your experience relate in any way to infant care? If yes, how?

3. What's wrong with creating the kind of teamwork in which the caregivers collectively care for all children by assigning tasks—one caregiver changes all diapers in the morning, and another feeds all the children breakfast, for example?

Chapter 6

Perception

Chapter 6 in your text focuses on perception. Though that word is never mentioned in this article, nevertheless sense perception is its main theme. In this issue of *Zero to Three*, where the theme is "The Multisensory World of the Infant," Tortora, who is a therapist in private practice, describes The Ways of Seeing program. She explains that this program uses the sensory-based experience of *seeing* as a metaphor to emphasize that there are many ways to look, assess, and receive information about self and others.

Reading 6

....

Our Moving Bodies Tell Stories, Which Speak of Our Experiences

Suzi Tortora

Dr. Suzi Tortora, a dance movement psychotherapist, is author of The dancing dialogue: Using the communicative power of movement with young children. *(2006) Baltimore: Paul H. Brookes Publishers.*

In the Ways of Seeing program, the practitioner is asked to become aware, through observation and interaction, of how nonverbal and multisensory-based experiences may influence an individual's experience. These individuals include oneself, children, and other family members who are involved in the child's intervention or educational program.

The core principles of this program state:

- Every individual creates a nonverbal movement style, based on multisensory experiences and composed of a unique combination of movement qualities.
- These qualities are the child's expressive/communicative style, regardless of how conventional or atypical that style may be.
- Skill and developmental levels are observed within the context of the quality of the child's nonverbal behaviors
- Even severe movement limitations have a qualitative element to them—it may be in the level of tension in their musculature, the position that the body habitually takes, or the frequency or lack of frequency of eye contact.
- How these qualities are expressed creates a sensation, an attitude, a response from the "mover" to those in the environment.

- In return, the observer of these behaviors has a reaction, based on their own experiences.
- This action-reaction influences the developing social/emotional relationship, and affects therapeutic and educational interventions.

Influenced by authentic movement practice developed by Adler[1], the Ways of Seeing practitioner is asked to monitor personal multisensory and nonverbal reactions through a specific self-observation process (Tortora,[2]). This involves: objectively mapping the details of the mover's actions (*witnessing*); becoming aware of and reflection upon her own sensorially based reactions (*kinesthetic seeing*); and becoming aware of and reflecting upon her emotional reactions, derived from experiencing interactions that include actually "trying on" the mover's actions (*kinesthetic empathy*). In this way of working, the practitioner takes a very active role during engagement with the child.

Becoming aware of and attuned to one's own multisensory reactions and responses has two functions. First, it enables the practitioner to become more open to the possible multisensory ways in which the child may be experiencing her surroundings. Young children initially explore, discover, and express themselves in their world primarily through their multisensory and nonverbal experiences. Second, the practitioner's self-monitoring of multisensory and nonverbal reactions enable her to become aware of the role she is playing in the developing relationship on a more subtle experiential level. Although nonverbal actions and reactions occur simultaneously with verbal and cognitive processing during communications and engagements with others, we tend not to register these reactions and modes of expression consciously. Much of the detail of sensorial and nonverbal communication is unconsciously recorded. It is essential to emphasize that the practitioner must be careful to view her observations as her own and not assume that they represent the child's experience, for one cannot truly know another's experience. The self-observation process expands the practitioner's attentiveness to this way of seeing, providing an added perspective to support the relationship and intervention.

Principles of a Session

Four principles guide each Ways of Seeing therapy session:

1. All activities in the session are structured to give the child the opportunity to use her multisensory-based, nonverbal movement style to show the practitioner who she is.
2. All nonverbal actions are regarded as having the potential to be communicative.
3. Nonverbal behaviors are expressions of self and have the potential to be used for meaningful communication.
4. The practitioner must always look through, behind, under, and over nonverbal behaviors, thinking, "What might this child be trying to tell me through these actions?"

The ability to regard all nonverbal actions as potential communications is a foundational aspect of this program, providing the practitioner with new ways to glean information about preverbal young children. This approach recognizes the communicative power of nonverbal gestures by going beyond "codified" nonverbal gestures, such as pointing and head-nodding, to observe uniquely personalized aspects of a child's movement style. This way of viewing nonverbal action requires the observer to pay attention the *qualitative* aspects of action.

· ·

---

[2] Adler, J. (1987, Winter). Who is witness? *Contact Quarterly Dance Journal, XII* (1), 20-29.

[3] Tortora, S. (1995, Winter). Seeing ourselves as a way to see young children. *Insights from the Center for Infants and Parents,* 2 (1), 4-7. New York: Teachers College, Columbia University.

Question about Reading 6

1. What are your reactions to this article?

2. This article combines the subjects of three chapters of your text: perception, motor skills, and communication. How does an infant communicate through movement?

3. If a child has severe movement limitations, how does he or she manage to communicate using the body?

Chapter 7

Motor Skills

This condensed excerpt focuses on the progression of movement development that occurs during the first two years of a child's life. It supplements the material on gross motor development in Chapter 7 of your text, giving details about what happens when children experience freedom of movement from birth on. The excerpt comes from Pikler's first book called *Peaceful Babies Contented Mothers,* which is based on her groundbreaking pre-World War II research on motor development. Today, her research is still new to most people and the methods it supports are quite different from those that restrict infant's movement, as is common in homes and child care centers across the United States. In this article she describes the development of movement in minute detail from birth to walking. Due to space, many of the details here have been summarized.

Reading 7

···

The Development of Movement

Emmi Pikler

As a pediatrician and researcher, Dr. Emmi Pikler's life and work were dedicated to infants. She was innovative in her approaches both as pediatrician and as founder of what is now called the Pikler Institute in Budapest, which is a residential nursery for infants and toddlers whose families cannot care for them. Her careful study of movement development is a legacy she passed on to us.

Note: Pikler advocated keeping infants on their backs until they could turn over by themselves, which was unheard of until the back-to-sleep campaign made the world aware of the dangers of tummy-sleeping (because of the risk of sudden infant death syndrome or SIDS). Since the 1990's most babies in the United States and elsewhere now spend a good deal of time on their backs, but are often propped up or put in restrictive devices. Pikler's approach is based on freedom of movement and she has plenty of evidence of the benefits of this approach in the quality of movement, excellent posture, and amazing balance that results. What follows is a very brief summary of the progression of movement development as she describes it.

The Child Is Born—Lies On the Back

A newborn infant lies on his back, with bent arms and legs, with closed fists, generally with the trunk and spine slightly bent to one side, the head turned a little sideward. The body, the way the infant is lying, is a little asymmetrical, and, often the two sides are not equally developed. Movements are abrupt, jerky, and accidental, without any purpose.

Turning the Head

The type of movement changes when an infant begins to follow an object of interest with her eyes and turns her head in a direction not previously practiced. The chaotic, hasty movements of the hands also change as soon as she begins to pay attention to the movement with her eyes. She observes her hands; we could even say she takes possession of them with her eyes. She discovers that these are her own hands. Under the constant guidance of her eyes she learns to move her hands with coordination and purpose.

Turning on the Side

When an infant is able to grasp well, he not only takes what happens to come into his hands, but stretches his arms more and more toward whatever interests him. Getting closer and closer to reaching the bedrails, he will gradually get pulled over onto his side. He can, however, also get over onto his side by turning the pelvis.

At first lying on the side is a big undertaking. Balance is insecure. We can see that, in the beginning, it is an effort for the infant to stay in that position. She is a bit stiff, supporting herself with her head, shoulder, arm, hand and feet. She returns often to lying on the back in order to rest. Later, after much practice, the child plays easily lying on her side. In this position, in contrast to lying on her back, she has a completely new and different view of things—including her hands. For weeks she plays, lying on her side.

Turning on the Belly

As soon as an infant is secure while lying on the side and playing—so secure that he no longer has to pay attention to balance—he may just lose that balance, fall over and land on the belly. Getting over onto the belly can also happen if the momentum of turning onto the side takes him too far, bringing him over onto the stomach. Usually an arm will get stuck under the trunk. That is, of course, unpleasant. The infant often starts crying. We want to help; we turn him over onto the back[1]—and, a few minutes later, find him on the belly again. We can help in the beginning, but we do not turn the infant over again each time—not even if he cries a little. If we know for sure that he did not get onto the belly accidentally, it is better to let him find his own solution. Sooner or later, he will help himself.

Stretching

Now the infant is able to move with intent. As surprising as it may seem, an infant, lying on the belly or on the back, seemingly unable to move anywhere at all, sooner or later will get near to the object or the playpen rails he is trying to reach. If the child is dressed, usually you will be unable to figure out how he did it. Only by observing the movement of a naked infant's body can you see what is actually happening. A child bends, stretches herself, makes minimal movements like a caterpillar. This slow and gradual stretching and reaching is one of the most important stages in the motor development of the infant. It goes on for months. During

---

1. Note that the infant is not helped onto his belly, but rather returned to his back. This is part of the principle of babies learning on their own with no help from adults. He is helped not to move forward, but merely put back in his original position for the purpose of getting his arm out from under him where it is stuck.

this time the asymmetry of the trunk with which the child is born disappears. Through these *natural* movements the spine becomes straight; the trunk becomes elastic, flexible and muscular.

I cannot emphasize how important this stage of development is. One proof is that the movements described above are systematically performed as special physical-therapy exercises with children who suffer from distortions of the spine. If infants were not forced to perform other kinds of movements (e.g., to sit up or stand up), and if sufficient space and time were given the children to move, then, day after day for many months, they would stretch themselves, tossing and turning, from the back onto the belly, from the belly onto the back.

Rolling

During the third quarter of the first year the infant is learning how to roll, from the back onto the belly and then from the belly onto the back—rolling on and on in one direction, moving safely and quickly from one place to another, reaching an object that caught his interest. Soon he will be able to roll well enough to go directly where he wants to go. At this time, an infant spends most of the day on her belly. With amazing skill she finds a posture which allows completely free movement of head, back, arms and legs. Sometimes the trunk is supported only on one point. She is kicking, slowly stretching, rolling—all day long, as she plays.

Creeping on the Belly and on all Fours

During the fourth quarter of the first year, the infant starts to creep on his belly. At first he usually slides backward instead of forward. Then he becomes more and more successful in moving forward. Sometimes the arms are more important in the action, sometimes the legs. Many children move forward using the arm-and-leg motions of swimming, as if they were doing the crawl-stroke. Sometimes they move so fast and skillfully that we adults could not keep pace with them if we wanted to move forward with the same motions. Each child creeps differently on the belly. It is not by chance that a child chooses a certain form, nor how long she practices different variations of a certain way of moving to get somewhere. As soon as she becomes strong through practice, she lifts herself into a hand-knee position. Later she begins to crawl on her hands and knees and, still late, eventually to walking on all fours, on the balls of her feet, like a bear. All this takes several months, during which time the child practices countless variations of these movements.

Children with weaker trunk-muscles move forward with their belly on the ground for a longer time. This strengthens the back and muscles of the trunk. Only after this do they crawl on all fours with the trunk lifted away from the ground. In time, these children, too, sit and stand up on their own, without our having sat or stood them up; it just happens later than average. If we are patient enough to wait for it to happen and if we do not urge them, they, too, will sit and stand straight.

It is clear that a child needs space to be able to crawl, more than there is in a little crib or a little playpen. Children will only develop as described above if they are given the opportunity to try out these movements *when they want to.*

Getting Up into the Vertical

The first attempts to stand up usually take place during the last quarter of the first year. A child <u>never</u> sits or stands up from the position of lying on his back. The sequence is always as I have described it. First he turns onto the belly. Then he begins to pull his knees in, etc. Normally, development from independently turning onto the belly to the beginnings of getting up takes five to six months. Starting in a secure prone position (on the stomach), he turns half onto the side, supported by one arm, and with the head lifted. In this way he comes to a half-sitting position. Later on he will sit up completely. Or he gets up onto his knees, then uses the sole of one foot for support, and then stands up. However, every movement in this process demands weeks or months of practice, like all the other sequences described.

Sitting

One could write long articles on sitting, on the different ways of sitting up, on correct and incorrect sitting. What in fact is the difference between "good" and "bad" sitting?

A child who sits well is able to move while sitting. She shifts her weight onto her sitting bones, her trunk rising up almost vertically on this basis. When she sits still, the area of the sacrum (lower back) is straight. The head is in line with, and a direct continuation of the back. That is the only way to sit without tiring. We are all acquainted with bad sitting. The entire trunk collapses into itself, the spine is bent, belly and chest are compressed, consequently the inner organs as well, and breathing becomes difficult. It is typical for us to be afraid that the child could suddenly fall over. Instead of putting her weight over her sitting bones—the parts of the pelvis meant for sitting—she sits behind them on the sacrum. In order to prevent herself from falling backward, she has to bend the whole upper part of her body very far forward.

Children try out the various kinds of positions in sitting, just as they have done in the other stages of their movement development. And when they have found a good state of balance and have mastered sitting, they will play in the sitting position—their backs straight—without overexerting themselves or getting exhausted.

Standing Up

Usually the child tries standing at the same time as sitting. It can happen that children stand up first, not sitting until later. In a kneeling position or rocking on the knees, they grasp the bars of their playpen or some other stable object and pull themselves up. At first they hardly rest on their feet, although they are standing. Clinging to something with their hands, they hold themselves up in a vertical position. To help support themselves, they may lean on something with their belly, pushing their lower back forward. At this moment many children experience their inability to get back down to the floor. If they get tired, they either let go of what they are holding and fall, or they hold on even tighter eventually starting to cry. Sometimes we help, but not all the time. The child can and will manage alone. Nothing serious can happen to her if she falls, even if she knocks her head a little. There are also children who are able to sit down again easily the very first time.

When they start to stand up, children put little weight on their feet. They often stand on tiptoe, with their legs spread apart. They don't stay in this position for long if there is an opportunity to crawl. They crawl off, stand up again somewhere else, crawl back again, etc. Gradually they stand more securely; they rest more of their weight on their feet and they use furniture less in standing up. The knees, which were stiff at first, begin to become elastic. Then the children straighten up; their lower back is no longer pushed forward. They don't cramp their hands anymore in holding onto something. The trunk as a whole can move more, is more supple.

Standing Up Alone—Without Holding On

For months children practice standing up before they can get up without holding onto anything. As they practice, they look like four-legged animals trying to stand up on their hind legs. They are very insecure at first, falling on their hands again and again until they succeed—for a few moments—in triumphantly remaining standing on both legs without holding on to anything. After a time, they stand up with a toy in their hands, and play in standing—more and more often without even noticing it. It usually takes four to six months for a child to learn to stand up, then to stand without holding on and finally to walk on his own. They need this time in order to become able to transfer the weight of their body to their feet with stability. Standing up without a support and walking alone take place in succession. All the time in between, if they aren't trying to stand, the children play, lying on the belly, sitting or crawling.

Walking About on their Own

In general, a child starts walking freely *during the first half of the second year*, if no one has interfered with her motor development. However, this is still more a matter of experimenting. Not until later will the child use walking instead of crawling for the purpose of moving from one place to another. A child who can already walk well will, for a long time, play mainly while squatting, kneeling or crawling. Many years later, children still like to kneel and squat when playing, if we do not forbid them to do this.

During the first phase of walking freely, children as a rule move with legs spread far apart and their feet turned far inward—insecure, like a sailor on a rocking boat—holding their arms like a tight-rope walker. They keep their balance with their hand, and try to clutch the ground with their feet, taking small steps, often lifting their knees up high. That lasts only a few days. Soon the necessary assurance has been reached. It seems that they walk with more ease, although the legs remain spread apart and the feet turned inward for many months, even for years. If their feet, knees and hips are weak and poorly built, the children continue walking this way for longer.

This, too, will correct itself if we are patient enough to wait. We do not interfere in the way the child moves, but continue to provide him at all times with the opportunity to move and play however he likes! We don't do anything to "straighten out" his legs or his gait. We let him walk with widespread legs as long as he is insecure, and with inward-turned feet as long as the soles of his feet are not yet strong! We allow a child to roll and crawl, even when she can already walk! We do not demand that she walk long distances!

For many more years a child whose legs are weak will tire easily, and move with a peculiar foot position. However, if we don't overstrain or make too great demands on the child, then the legs will become stronger and, without anyone making corrections or interfering, the feet will adjust their position to be more toward the front. The legs come closer together, the walking becomes beautiful and secure, the child as a whole has more endurance.

....

Questions about Reading 7

1. Emmi Pikler spent nearly a lifetime observing and studying infants and toddlers movement development. She clearly trusts children to develop on their own without help (she used the term interference) from adults. You may have some reactions to reading about infants left to develop on their own without ever being put into a position they can't get into by themselves. What are your thoughts and feelings after reading this article?

2. What is not in this article is what happens during caregiving times. If someone just left children to develop on their own, without any relationship, the picture would be very different. Movement development only occurs in the Pikler Institute because the babies have a close trusting relationship with one or more caregivers. They aren't just left on their own the whole time. They have an adult they can depend on and also develop peer relationships. However, using the Pikler approach means that infants learn to move on their own, without adult interference—so infants' interactions with adults take place mainly during caregiving times. What are your thoughts and feelings about adults using caregiving times as the main focus of interactions with infants, instead of interacting with infants throughout the day?

Chapter 8

Cognition

In Chapter 8 of your text, you'll find a section on pretend play. When children play pretend, they are able to make mental representations and use symbols by using one thing to stand for another. Miller's article explains how infants use symbols long before they reach the stage of playing pretend, which has significance for mental development and is a sign that they are already engaged in some of the learnings of early literacy.

Reading 8

How Infants and Toddlers Use Symbols

Karen Miller

Karen Miller is the author of (among other titles) Simple Steps: Developmental Activities for Infants, Toddlers and Twos *and the revised version of* Things to Do with Toddlers and Twos.

There is a piece of cognitive development that we usually don't pay too much attention to with infants and toddlers: the use of symbols. Here's how my desk dictionary (TIME: Webster's New Deal Dictionary, 1978) defines symbol:

1) Something that stands for something else; especially something concrete that represents or suggests another thing that cannot in itself be represented or visualized. 2) A letter, character, or sign used (as to represent a quantity, position, relationship, direction, or something to be done) instead of a word or group of words.

Our technological society is built around symbols. Reading and writing, mathematics, finance, and science all require that an individual is adept at using symbols.

In one sense, educators often make the mistake of trying to force children to use symbols too early, before they are ready for abstract concepts. We see this when well-meaning parents spend much time showing children flash cards of words, or teachers drill children on the alphabet. On the other hand, symbols are present in children's natural play almost from the beginning. If we understand how they use symbols, we can give them good opportunities to *grow the skill*.

Action Symbols

A newborn, of course, does not come into the world knowing how to use symbols. Very early on, however, this new human being is learning how to *read* symbols in the environment. An impending action can

Reprinted with permission from *Child Care Information Exchange*, PO Box 3249, Redmond, WA 98073, (800) 221-2864. *www.ChildCareExchange.com.*

be represented by a symbol. A siren, for example, is a symbol that tells us we will soon see a speeding vehicle and we should get out of the way.

Very young infants quickly learn symbols for when something is about to happen. Here's one that is easy to recognize: you reach toward the child with your arms to pick him up, and the baby stiffens his neck and moves a little toward you, or even reaches his arms out to you, indicating that he has *read* the symbol of your posture. There are other symbols of daily routines you could probably think of: putting coats on = going outside; the smell of food being fed and satiating hunger; telephone rings at home = interruption of interaction with the child.

What we can do:

- Always approach the child from the front and use the same gesture of putting your arms out when you are about to pick up the child. Also use the word symbols to go with this gesture. "Up . . ." or, "I'm going to pick you up now."
- Create other consistent symbols. Play certain, calming music or a particular lullaby when you put the child down to nap; tap on the bowl when you are about to feed the child; or always take the child to the same chair when you are about to give the child a bottle.
- With toddlers, play certain music at clean-up time, ring a small bell when it is snack time, bring out a particular puppet when it is time for a story.

What else can you think of? All of these symbols help the child read the environment and know what is going to happen next. That helps a child feel secure and in control.

Object Symbols

First of all, before we even talk about symbols, give the child lots of experience playing with safe objects of all kinds. The child must handle and mouth objects of all shapes and materials simply to *get the feel* of the physical world. In so doing, the child learns about the properties of shapes, materials, and textures. This helps the child to form a firm image in his mind. The phenomenon of *object hunger* dominates children's play from about the age of six months to 18 months. It is the famous *into everything* stage. The children are on an obsessive quest to touch and become acquainted with every object within sight . . . and not necessarily within immediate reach!

Another cognitive phenomenon that occurs at this time which has a close connection to the ability to see objects as symbols is *object permanence*. The child learns to create and maintain a mental image of an object that is out of sight as she searches for it. Objects, especially toys, can be symbols that represent something else. When a child has learned to keep the image of an object in her mind she will also be more able to look at a toy and see the larger, real thing that the toy object represents.

I first became aware of a toddler's ability to see toys as a symbol when I watched a 20 month old lie down on a 4" long dollhouse bed. It's true that a toddler doesn't really know how big his body is, but I don't think this toddler was that confused. What he was really doing is saying by his actions, "I know what this small piece of wood represents." Other examples are toy telephones, toy steering wheels, dolls, and various doll accessories. We often see children even under one year of age pick up such objects and show that they know what the thing it represents is used for.

This is the first seed of dramatic play, using objects as symbols. Later, the child will begin to take on a role and interact with others within that role. But for now, just using a toy object in an appropriate way indicates that the child understands what it symbolizes.

What we can do:

- Give young infants plenty of free time on the floor and many safe and interesting objects of all types to examine.

- Find toys that represent things in the child's world and make them available.
- Play along. If the child hands you the toy phone, for example, talk into it.

Picture Symbols

A picture is a symbol of a three-dimensional object. We know that one of the first steps in learning to read is reading the illustrations in a picture book. The child must see that the arrangement of lines and shapes on the page symbolizes something real. One prerequisite that people, even those who write and illustrate books for this age, sometimes forget, is that the child must be familiar with the object before the picture will be meaningful. If the child has never seen an elephant, the small shape on the page will not give the child an accurate image of the thing.

What we can do:

- Find pictures of things in the child's environment. Talk about them as you show them to the child. Compare them to the object that is present.
- Glue pictures of objects in the environment to individual cards. Hand the card to the child. See if the child can bring the card over to the object it represents.
- Create photo experience books. Take pictures when the children are engaged in something memorable, like playing with bubbles or going for a walk. Put these photos in a little book, or on a piece of posterboard. Then look at the photos together and talk about them. The children will learn to connect the images to real things and happenings.
- Make a visual discrimination poster. Glue pictures of many of the toys you have in the room on one piece of posterboard. (Out of date supplier catalogs are a good source for the pictures.) Then bring a toy over to the poster and ask the child, "Where is the picture of this toy? Can you find it?"

Books

Books, of course, are a whole system of picture symbols as well as word symbols that represent objects, actions, and experiences. When you choose books for your program, be very conscious of the quality of the illustrations as well as their relevance to the child's life. When you read to very young children, what you are mostly doing is helping them with picture identification. You follow their lead and allow them to point to pictures and name them. They delight in finding an object you name on the page in front of them.

What we can do:

- Gather together some of the objects represented by pictures in the book. First, let the child see the pictures, then play with the real objects. After reading *Pots and Pans* by Patricia Hubbell (Harper Growing Tree), for instance, let the child use wooden spoons to beat on a real pot.
- Do some of the activities represented in a book. For instance, if there is cooking in the book, do some cooking with the children.

Language Development and Symbols

Words are symbols, of course. The more words a child acquires, the more adept he becomes at using symbols. Words provide handles or anchors for thoughts. So everything you do to enhance language development encourages cognitive development. Talk to children. Read to them. Describe what they are seeing and doing. Listen to them and be patient in their attempts to speak. Let them know that their language has power.

Why Should We Be Thinking about the Ages and Stages of Symbol Use?

Many children spend their first three years in an impoverished environment when it comes to learning to use symbols. The modem day culprit is, no news here, television. Television is really all symbols, you might rightly say. But they are the wrong type of symbol at the wrong time. They are too fast, and too abstract. Rather than showing a connection to real life, they are often simply mesmerizing as the child stares at moving patterns. Make sure that the children in your program do not lead a boring life, trapped in swings and such, or randomly playing without much quality adult interaction.

A simple awareness could go a long way to enhancing this aspect of your program. Delight when you see children interpreting some subtle symbol. Tell the parents about it. Invent new symbols, and build on what you already do.

. . . .

Questions about Reading 8

1. Is Miller describing curriculum and lessons as Lally sees them? As you see them? Explain.

2. Can you find some "mini-lessons" in Miller's article? If yes, describe them.

3. Can you think of an "action symbol" that is different from the examples Miller gives? Write it below.

4. Some toddlers enjoy informal and spontaneous "matching games." Can you find some examples in Miller's article of what could be called "matching games"? What do you think is the point of helping a child notice what matches what?

Chapter 9

Language

Early Literacy is part of Chapter 9 in your text; however, the chapter focuses more on language than on literacy because the message is that language development is the foundation of literacy. There is no literacy without language. Ruth Anne Hammond makes that point and goes on to add key pieces of the philosophy on which your text is based, such as involving the child in caregiving routines, maintaining slow pace, and allowing freedom of movement. Watch how far she goes beyond just talking to children when she addresses language as the foundation of literacy.

Reading 9

Preparing for Literacy: Communication Comes First

Ruth Anne Hammond

Ruth Anne Hammond is a Master Teacher at Pacific Oaks, Infant/Toddler-Parent Center, and served as president on the RIE Board of Directors from 2005–2011.

It is not uncommon to hear a new parent proudly exclaim of her 20 month old, "She already knows her ABC's!" It is true that the parent has a right to be proud…but not for the reason she thinks! Usually children of toddler age who "know" their ABC's are simply displaying the fact that they have had "The Alphabet Song" sung to them so many times that they have memorized (what sounds to them like) a very long string of nonsense syllables. Often children well beyond the toddler stage can be heard asking, "'What's an 'elemeno'?" This gives evidence that just because a child can repeat the sounds of the alphabet, she does not yet understand that the sounds represent letters, which in turn, represent the sounds in words. For most children, these understandings come a bit later than age two, or even age three.

However, what the parent above should be congratulated on is that she has been spending time and singing with her child. The interactive repetition of the simple songs and nursery rhymes of early childhood are an important aid in helping young children recognize new words, and also in identifying the discrete sounds within words. As an example, "The Eeensy Weensy Spider" is just as helpful in building the foundation for literacy as "The Alphabet Song."

There are a number of other ways in which we can help build a strong foundation for literacy (and these are the same methods we at Pacific Oaks Infant/Toddler Parent Center recommend to parents). We speak to children about what concerns them, and listen patiently for their responses. Oral language is the first step toward symbolic representation; a spoken (or signed) word is a symbol for an object, attribute or action.

Thus a written word is a symbol of a symbol. What precedes such complex abstraction is meaningful communication. Being surrounded by caring people, who speak clearly and listen respectfully, helps young children develop their desire to communicate.

Building in plenty of patience for a toddler's slower-than-adult response time is essential. The key to effective communication with infants and toddlers is to *slow down* and to involve them in all caregiving routines such as diapering or feeding. The messages exchanged in 5000 diaper changes or 3000 feeding times surely add up! We pay attention to what interests the children, and speak with them about those things.

The best learning experiences are those that have a positive emotional charge. For a toddler, "positive emotional charge" translates as fun. Therefore, meeting children at their interests is the key to building meaningful vocabulary. What creates this positive emotional charge in the Pacific Oaks Infant/Toddler program? You guessed it! Water and sand and climbing and garbage trucks and baby dolls and dumping/filling. You get the picture: Lots of choices, lots of sensory experiences, lots of freedom to choose.

We also giver toddlers freedom to move on their own. Gross-motor development plays an important role in brain development. A child who spends too much time strapped in an infant seat, car seat, walker or other restraining device is being deprived of the opportunity to develop bilateral connections in the brain, which may impact other types of learning. And in spite of the fact that parents often think getting babies upright (as in a walker or baby seat) increases the visual stimulation they are receiving, the babies actually receive the opposite of the desired effect. Recent research shows that infants who spend time in walkers score lower on intelligence tests later in childhood. A baby needs access to her whole range of postures and transitional movements if her brain is to develop optimally. It is important at this point to note that children who have limited movement options due to special needs can certainly become good readers. The point is that all children benefit from the freedom to move within their capacities.

We also provide the chance to look at books that are meaningful to children's lives. As we set up the play areas, we set out a toy such as a green toy tractor and place next to it a book about tractors. This provides a chance for each toddler to abstract to that next level of symbolic thought, (real tractor, toy tractor, picture of a tractor, and later, the word, "tractor") as well as to have conversations (verbal and nonverbal) with whatever adult may be there to read with that child.

We're not so much looking for children to begin to recognize specific printed words (although many toddlers seem to be reading as they parrot back what has been repeatedly read to them), but for them to begin to associate books with warm, close interactions with adults, and to expand their knowledge base about the world. We are much less concerned with children finishing a book than in the conversation the book inspires. It is a pure pleasure to read this way with a child—even if it's for the twenty-fifth time! Repetition is *very* important at this age!

Supporting the joy of discovery is our primary goal because the most important foundation for all kinds of academic success is the love of learning. A toddler who is busy rediscovering the world and inventing him-or herself is on the road to a lifetime of expanding opportunity. This will eventually, no doubt, include plenty of reading both for enlightenment and for pleasure.

Questions about Reading 9

1. What does the author of this article think is good about a toddler knowing the ABC's? Do you agree with the article?

2. What do you remember about learning to read? What do you think happened to you in your early years that provided the foundation for your learning to read? Does your experience relate to the article?

3. What does it mean that learning experiences for infants and toddlers should have a positive emotional charge? Can you think of a learning experience in your own life that had a positive emotional charge?

Chapter 10

Emotions

Chapter 10 on emotions discusses the strong pull that infant emotions can have on adult feelings. This article is about helping a baby adjust to center care and how its author, Elliot, had to put aside what she already knew from years of experience and focus just on this baby in this situation. The article is about what she learned. You may remember that in Chapter 2 your text examined attachment issues, including separation, which is the subject of this article.

Reading 10

....

Helping a Baby Adjust to Center Care

Enid Elliot

Enid Elliot, Ph.D. is an instructor of early childhood education with Pacific Rim Early Childhood Institute in Victoria, British Columbia, Canada, and a research associate in the School of Child and Youth Care at the University of Victoria. She has helped set up and run an infant program based in a school program for young women.

Once in a while a false sense of security creeps over me. Life in the infant/toddler care program gets quiet, and any problems that do crop up are easily solved. 1 even start to categorize babies and mothers: each new family reminds me of a previous family. I begin to feel like an expert. Then comes a baby who cannot be categorized.

Several years ago we had such a baby at a child care center I supervised. Our usual tricks of the trade did not work. By challenging our assumptions about how to care for three-month-old infants, we eventually arrived at a successful solution. This took observation, thought, and commitment to the baby and her mother.

Since then I have thought often about Serena and her mother, Krista. Serena seemed to contradict the child development texts I had studied. Theorists tell us that babies do not develop stranger anxiety until the second half of their first year. As Barton and Williams note, "Data from the few studies that have looked at age of enrollment suggest that infants enrolled in substitute care during the first half of the first year are less vulnerable to disturbances in the attachment relationship than infants enrolled in substitute care in the second half of the first year" (1993, 452).

In my work I am aware of the usefulness of theories and of their limitations. Serena's story reminded me once again to be careful of making too many assumptions about babies. Theories do apply to most children, but it is also important to remember that every child is an individual.

An Alternative Program for Young Mothers and Babies

Options Daycare is part of the Girls' Alternative Program (GAP) of the public school system in Victoria, British Columbia. GAP is for pregnant teens and young mothers who need an alternative to the regular school system. The school and the child care staff work as a team to help the young mothers balance their academic and parenting responsibilities. GAP provides an individualized academic program for young mothers, so a student is not penalized, for example, if her baby is sick and she must take time off.

Options serves 12 babies: four caregivers look after the babies while their supervisor supports them in a multitude of ways. Usually six younger infants are in one group, with six older infants, 9 to 18-plus months, in another. We keep an anecdotal log on each baby as well as photos and videos The log is used to communicate with the mother about her baby's day; It is informal and, understandably, positive in tone.

Our Experience with One Baby—A Case Study

When I began to recall our experiences with Serena. I had her anecdotal record and video to work from. I interviewed Serena's mother and her former caregiver to get a fuller picture. This case study is based on the interviews and a review of the informal written and videotape records covering a 10-month period. September to June. The names of everyone involved have been changed.

Serena's arrival

It was Options' third year of operation with the same group of caregivers when three-month-old Serena arrived at the center. We worked well as a team, employing a coherent philosophy of sensitive and responsive caregiving. Each baby was assigned a primary caregiver who established the main relationship with both mother and child. Children stayed with their caregivers. if at all possible, throughout their two years in the program.

The staff worked as primary caregivers within a team framework. Our team had solved a number of problems together and felt that the babies developed a sense of security and well-being in our program. Our approach was to observe and respond sensitively to each baby. We worked at creating a calm and unhurried atmosphere.

Her family

Krista had been in GAP while she was pregnant. When her baby was born. she continued in school and brought Serena to the child care center. Krista was a very sociable 18-year-old who liked school and did well in her classes.

Krista gave birth to Serena on June 12, two weeks early. She weighed five pounds, eight ounces. Krista lived in a group home with Serena and other young mothers and their babies. Serena's father Don was very attentive, involved in her life from the beginning. In November Don and Krista moved in together (and subsequently married). Both parents were very attached to Serena. Her father regularly spent time with her at child care.

Serena's primary caregiver, Harriet

At three months Serena started our program at the beginning of the school year in September. Her primary caregiver, Harriet, had met Serena at a drop-in program we ran during summer vacation. Harriet recalls that six-week-old Serena was not comfortable when she first held her then, relaxing only when she was returned to her mother.

From a very young age. Serena preferred her mother to all others and was often anxious when separated from her. Experience had taught us that when babies enter the child care center at three months old. they have a period of adjustment as they become accustomed to our environment and their assigned caregiver. It also takes time for the caregiver to adjust to a baby's rhythms. But the transition for three-month-old infants tends to be smoother than for older infants, who are often more accustomed to a home routine or setting. Younger babies seem able to respond to the sensitive caregiving provided by our program. However, it took Serena more than six months to adjust and to feel comfortable with Harriet.

Our Review and Reflection on the Events

Early on, Harriet's notes in the communication log describe Serena as a wriggler. When we review the videotape we see a petite, nicely chubby baby. She moves steadily, her legs up and arms waving. But there is an anxious expression on her face. She watches people and events around her with focused concentration.

Harriet remembers Serena as a tense baby who was very alert. Both she and Krista comment on a sound— ging—that four-month-old Serena repeated when distressed. They recall that when she was upset, Krista was very effective in calming her; indeed she was the only one who could.

Throughout the fall we waited for Serena to settle in. We wondered, why hasn't Serena responded to the separation anxiety strategies that work well with other babies? The mothers were just down the hall, and their teachers were used to the caregivers calling them to come and feed or settle their babies. Krista nursed Serena. but we also fed her by bottle. We fetched Krista often, whenever Serena was distressed. She preferred the breast and her mother.

Trying various strategies

Krista became frustrated by the frequent interruptions. We attempted to give her a break by trying several things we thought might help Serena relax and allow us to begin to meet her needs. We tried reducing stimulation by wrapping her tightly, even covering her head with a blanket when she was tired and needed to sleep. We put a steamer in the nap room to create white noise that cut down on the distracting noise from the school and the child care program. We hoped she could stay asleep once she fell asleep.

Krista used a pacifier with Serena. While Serena took the soother from her mother, she did not like to take it from Harriet. We tried a variety of ideas: however, not wanting a baby to be in distress for long, we usually ended up getting her mom. As Krista recalls, Serena could be hyperventilating when she arrived, but as soon as she picked her up, her baby would stop and relax. Serena found comfort only in her mother's presence.

Krista was a very caring mom, but she could see that other babies were adjusting to the center, and she felt bad that Serena wasn't making a smooth transition. She had a clear commitment to her daughter. This was a frustrating situation for Krista and for everyone else. But we were optimistic that Serena would eventually settle down and feel comfortable.

By the end of September, when Serena arrived in the mornings with her mother, she would look happily at the other children and the toys. On a videotape she is seen watching a one-year-old with intense interest. But while Serena seemed to like coming, she became anxious as soon as her mother left. Some days she coped by fussing but usually she lost all restraint and wailed. "It was she panicked." says Harriet. If she fell asleep, it was usually only a light sleep that was not very restful.

Furthering our attempts to comfort

By the end of October, we decided to lengthen the time spent responding to Serena before getting Krista. We used swaddling, stimulation reduction, rocking, and crooning; we took Serena outside, hoping fresh air would calm her. Each strategy worked for a bit, only to prove ineffective in the long run. We hoped that Serena was absorbing the message that we were dependable and trying to help her, even if we did not always find the right moves. When she was unhappy, we tried to listen and understand.

The process was wearing. Serena screamed, often for as long as 45 minutes at a time. She had good days, but might still slip into a panic that only her mother could address. It was a delicate balance. Harriet remembers being on pins and needles, never knowing when Serena would start to cry. Then there would be no stopping her until she was exhausted or we got Krista.

By December we were all unhappy with the situation. Krista thought she was not meeting Serena's needs and felt confused, not knowing what those needs were. Harriet, feeling like a failure, thought. "This job is not for me."

I was puzzled too. Why wasn't anything working? We were an organized, uncrowded center with highly skilled staff, yet we had not come up with a solution for Serena. We considered medical problems. but the doctor assured us that Serena was healthy. We wondered if she was getting enough to eat. She nursed only for short periods but fairly often, and she did not eagerly accept a bottle. She was small but not skinny.

With the holidays coming, Krista and Don planned to go away for a quiet time by themselves with Serena. A break would be welcome! We hoped that after vacation matters would sort themselves out,as they often do. Then Krista's grandmother died, and Krista and Serena traveled east for the funeral to be with her family.

The trip was traumatic for Serena. Krista says. Hers is a large family, with lots of commotion and everyone wanting to hold the baby. Without Don. and in strange surroundings, Krista believes. Serena was overwhelmed. She also had a cold, which developed into bronchitis.

Finally!—The Plan that Worked

When Serena and Krista returned in January, the situation at the center did not improve at all. We developed a new plan. This time we took the advice of Magda Gerber. From her work with infants in the Loczy Institute, Gerber (1979) says that if things are very consistent, infants learn to know that they are, for instance, always the third one to be fed and thus can tolerate the wait.

We decided to start anew, and we asked Krista to begin by spending much of her time in the center for a while. Our hope was that we could get Serena to count on her mom's presence as a secure base and then that the feeling would extend to being in child care without her mom.

Each morning Krista arrived at about nine and spent an hour settling Serena: changing her diaper, feeding her pablum, nursing, and sitting close by while the baby played. Then Krista had an hour away. She would meet with her teacher, then return and stay until one o'clock when she had another half-hour break. This schedule was possible because our program was in an alternative education program. Each young woman worked at her own pace. The school supported our child care program in its process; we had discussed our concerns and plans together.

What was happening?

In the log Harriet had noted, "It's now been two days that our plan has been in effect, and I can already see changes in Serena. She seems much happier; her cry seems less panicky than usual."

A month later, after both mother and child were out sick for a week, Harriet wrote. "Welcome back, guys. Glad to see you're both feeling better. Serena had a good day today. She seemed quite pleased to be back and played happily all day. She sure has grown since the last time I saw her. . . . It seems to me that Serena is feeling much safer and secure, so tomorrow we can start the new schedule, which will allow you more time for school, Krista." Gradually Krista took longer times away from the center.

While Krista hung out in the baby corner with Serena, Harriet established a closer relationship with Krista. Together they played games with the baby. Harriet sat close to Krista so Serena could see them together. They played peekaboo games and encouraged Serena to go from one lap to the other. Harriet's goal was to become associated in Serena's mind with Krista.

Progress is evident

On March 2 Harriet wrote, "Serena had a wonderful day today. She seemed quite cheerful and content all day. It's so wonderful to see how safe she feels here. She plays happily, exploring every possible little corner of the babies' side of the infant/toddler room. Every once in a while when she starts getting upset, she makes her way over to me for a reassuring hug, and then she's off again. She really is a wonderful little girl. Once again I must commend you, Krista. All your hard work paid off."

By May, Harriet noted that Serena was even beginning to go to other staff. She was making the transference from her mother to Harriet and then to other caregivers. From this point on, the picture is that of a baby who was developing well, relaxed and secure in her setting.

It took from September to March for us to say that Serena had settled in. At three months old she had wanted her mother and did not easily accept a substitute. But by the end of March, after seven months, our 10-month-old Serena was part of the program. She reminded us to stay alert to each baby and to each situation. Some situations are familiar and easily solved while others require thought and creativity.

Harriet continued as Serena's primary caregiver. She remembers Serena as a child who was "sensitive to everything." Harriet expands on this description by recounting an incident from Serena's toddlerhood, after she had settled happily into child care. One afternoon while Serena napped, the staff moved a shelf to a more convenient place. After waking up, Serena came out of the nap room and stopped in the middle of the room. She looked around and tears started to roll down her cheeks. Harriet asked her what was wrong, but Serena just continued to cry, looking apprehensive. Finally it dawned on Harriet that the room change had upset Serena. Harriet and the staff moved the shelf back to its original place and changed it later when Serena was awake and involved.

Discussion and Conclusions

I had not expected a three-month-old baby to react to her mother's absence with such tenaciousness. It seemed that Serena was actively seeking her mother as she fussed and cried and our efforts to comfort her only increased her determination to get to her mother. It took persistence on our part to discover a solution that facilitated Serena's attachment to Harriet, her caregiver.

Our support of this baby, caregiver, and mother took time and energy, and fortunately our program is set up to provide extended time and individualized care. This experience convinced me that some babies need very careful nurturing as they make the transition to child care.

I worry about the babies who attend busy centers with a higher child-to-adult ratio. How do overworked center staff respond to infants like Serena? How do babies who are alert, sensitive, and slow to include the caregiver in their attachment system cope with caregivers who do not have time to listen to their concerns?

Greta Fein notes that "some infants enter child care with dispositions associated with poor developmental outcomes in home-reared infants. . . . However, the quality of interaction provided by caregivers is crucial. Conceivably, well-trained and interactive caregivers can modulate the distress most infants experience when they enter child care. Inhibited, self-soothing infants may be especially vulnerable because they are easy to ignore even in relatively high-quality child care settings" (1995, 274). Harriet's role in Serena's adjustment to the center was key; yet like most caregivers. she also needed support to keep actively engaged in the process.

Kagan and Snidman estimate that 10 percent of infants are "vulnerable to a specific form of anxiety that is generated by unfamiliar people, settings, or challenges" (1991, 858). These children, whom they call inhibited, show high levels of motor activity and crying in response to novelty at four months of age and do not welcome change, new people, or strange situations.

Research indicates that infants, like adults, have different temperaments (Thomas & Chess 1977). As caregivers we have a responsibility to respond to each child as an individual. We must take time to observe, ponder the meaning of what we see, and explore the best possible approach for each baby and family.

Consistent evidence suggests that quality care encourages optimal child development (Howes & Olenick 1986; Howes. Phillips. & Whitebook 1992). The National Day Care Study (Ruopp et al. 1979) identified group size, child-to-staff ratios, and caregiver training as significant predictors of both caregiver behavior and child outcome. "Larger group sizes and higher child-to-staff ratios were associated with more restrictive and management-focused staff behavior, with diminished social interaction and language stimulation between staff and children, and with increased apathy and overt distress among infants" (Barton & Williams 1993, 456).

Because we keep both group size and the child-to-staff ratios low at Options, we can focus on the babies and their mothers. Within a small group a level of intimacy and trust is reached that is not possible in a larger group. Caregivers must be sensitive and involved; they must particularly be "self-reflective and expert in their field" (Howes & Hamilton 1993, 30). We must protect and support our caregivers so they have the time and energy to reflect and respond with sensitivity to the infants in their care. Harriet benefited from our frequent daily meetings, which were crucial to maintaining her sense of competence. Serena's was a situation that would have tested anyone's sense of efficacy. Staff collaborated with Harriet to develop strategies. Collaboration like this should be built into the daily operations of any quality program, along with crucial inservice staff development and support (Hopkins 1990).

It is also Important to give infants consistent care. There is a high staff-turnover rate in the field of early childhood education. It may take time to settle an infant like Serena into a program. and that process is seriously disrupted by a change in caregivers (Raikes 1993). Ensuring that caregivers have the knowledge, skills, and support they need to perform their jobs should increase the probability of infants doing well in nonfamilial care.

Epilogue

It was four years later when I worked with Krista on this account of Serena's adjustment to the center. She said she was unaware it had been so difficult from the beginning. Later, when talking to a friend who had known Serena from birth, she heard a new story. The friend had cared for five-month-old Serena when Don and Krista went out for an evening. Serena had been upset and inconsolable. The friend called her own mother, a nurse, who suggested that she wear something that smelled like Krista. She put on Krista's makeup so Serena could smell the familiar scent while being held. Only then did Serena fall asleep.

I enjoyed meeting Serena at five years old, a little girl with an open, sunny manner. The small baby with the bald head—slow to get hair—was now a beautiful child with lovely auburn hair. Greeting me with curiosity and warmth, she showed me a well-thumbed child care scrapbook. As I talked with her mom, Serena listened with great interest to stories of her babyhood.

As I left, Serena gave me a large baby photo of herself to show to Harriet. When I returned the photo some time later and told her that Harriet had said hello, she grinned and wriggled with delight.

Questions about Reading 10

1. Serena was unhappy in child care for six months. What are some of the methods the primary caregiver and other staff used to try to soothe her? Can you think of any they didn't try?

2. Have you ever been in a situation where a baby you were with just couldn't be soothed? What did you do? How did you feel? What did you think?

3. What in the article told you that the feelings centered on separation anxiety, not just from being in a new environment?

Chapter 11

Social Skills

Chapter 11 on socialization focuses a good deal on toddlers, because as babies begin to move around, their world expands and socialization becomes important. This article is becoming a classic, one that teachers and directors have on file and pull out every year for a handout in a class or a staff meeting.

Reading 11

....

Toddlers: What to Expect

Janet Gonzalez-Mena

Janet Gonzalez-Mena is retired from Napa Valley College, Napa, California and is now an early childhood consultant and writer

Which of these paragraphs best describes toddlers?

Toddlers don't sit still for a minute. They have short attention spans and are highly distractible. They always want their own way, and won't share or take turns. Toys always get lost or broken when toddlers play with them.

Toddlers are active explorers. They eagerly try new things and use materials in different ways. Toddlers want to be independent and they have a strong sense of ownership.

The first description compares toddlers with older children and looks at typical toddler behavior in negative terms. The second is a positive outlook that respects toddlers and their natural behavior.

When teachers or parents think of toddlers as miniature preschoolers, we run into problems because our expectations are not appropriate. For example, inappropriate expectations can turn toilet learning into a struggle of wills between adult and child. Meals can be chaotic because toddlers play with their food. Circle time can be a nightmare because toddlers keep wandering around or interrupting. Adult-directed activities get disrupted as toddlers choose their own ways instead of following what the teacher has in mind. Puzzles get dumped, toys are pulled off shelves and hauled to another area of the room, and verbal attempts to intervene are ignored as toddlers go about their business.

What can parents or teachers of toddlers do, either at home or in group programs, to work effectively with toddlers? Few parents have any background in child development, and many teachers have been prepared to work with older children. What are the differences between toddlers and preschoolers, and how can we make the most of these often maligned months of early childhood?

What Toddlers Are Like

Toddlers learn with their whole bodies—not just their heads. They learn more through their hands than they do through their ears. They learn by doing, not only by just thinking. They learn by touching, mouthing, and trying out, not by being told.

Toddlers solve problems on a physical level. Watch toddlers at play for just 5 minutes and you will see them walk (which looks like wandering), climb, carry things around, drop things, and continually dump whatever they can find. These large muscle activities are not done to irritate adults—they are the legitimate activity of toddlers. Piaget calls this the sensorimotor stage of development (1952, 1954).

Toddlers can become absorbed in discovering the world around them. If you are convinced that toddlers have short attention spans, just watch them with running water and a piece of soap. Handwashing can become the main activity of the morning! Eating is another major activity, as many toddlers switch from neat to very messy in a short time. Filling and dumping are great skills to use with food or water. Of course, toddlers do put things in as part of the process, but they are more likely to end with dumping! Other toddlers are reluctant to mess around in their food once they can handle utensils well.

In addition to these primarily cognitive and physical skills, toddlers are also working on a number of socioemotional challenges. They are still developing trust in the adults who care for them, so parents and teachers need to work closely to help children learn how to cope with important events such as separation.

Toddlers are in Erikson's second stage—autonomy (1963). Their rapidly emerging language clearly demonstrates what it means to be autonomous: "Me do it" shows the drive for independence. "Me-mine!" indicates toddlers are beginning to see themselves as individuals with possessions. And, of course, the "NO!" toddlers are so famous for is a further clue to their push for separateness and independence.

Some of the major accomplishments of this stage of growing independence are self-help skills such as dressing, feeding, washing, and toileting. All of these skills involve a great deal of practice, and the inevitable mishaps. Learning to use the toilet, like all the other self-help skills, is a physical feat, as well as an intellectual and emotional one. It takes time for the child to gain physical control, to understand what to do, and to be willing to do it.

With all of these major accomplishments emerging during toddlerhood—from approximately 14 months to 3 years of age—what, then, should toddlers do all day, at home or in a group program?

Some Common Pitfalls

Both parents and teachers have been influenced by the push to demonstrate that children are *learning* something. Those who are unfamiliar with the remarkable natural learnings of the toddler period often feel compelled to create so-called learning activities as proof that the adult is teaching the child.

These activities often become part of a curriculum such as one I observed. For the first 45 minutes, the teacher helped children cope with separation as their parents said goodbye. The children were helped to remove their coats and hang them up, diapers were changed, and some children used the toilet. The children playing with toys argued, got frustrated, or asked for adult help. What a pleasure it was to see a program responding to the variety of learnings so much a part of toddlerhood—separation and trust, self-help skills and autonomy, and problem solving through hands-on play experiences.

Just then a bell rang, and the children were herded into a group, organized, separated into smaller groups, seated at tables, and given what were termed learning activities to do. Later, the director apolo-

Table 1 Preschool activities that can be modified for toddlers	
Preschool activity	**Modified toddler activity**
Easel painting	Water on chalkboards
Paint and paper	Thick soap suds with food coloring on Plexiglas™
Sponge painting	Squeeze sponges in trays with a little water on the bottom
Cooking with recipes	Cutting or mashing bananas or similar one-step food experience
Pasting tissue paper	Crumpling white tissue paper (to prevent dyes from running colors when chewed)

gized: "We were late in getting started," she explained. For her, the valuable time was the organized activity time, not the 45 minutes when toddlers were involved in taking steps toward the major accomplishments of toddlerhood!

Of course, toddlers learn from activities, just as they learn from any experience—but activities are *not* more valuable than the rest of what happens in a typical day at home or in a program. Most importantly, *activities are only valuable to the degree to which they are appropriate for the age group.*

If the activities are too advanced—perhaps requiring toddlers to sit at tables, to wait 10 minutes for their turn, or to color in the spaces of an adult's drawing—children will learn to limit and restrict themselves, to feel unsuccessful, to sense a lack of respect for themselves as individuals. An opportunity for children to explore with their senses in more creative ways will have been lost.

Sometimes traditional preschool activities can be modified for toddlers. For example, given collage materials, many toddlers will experiment by licking the glue, eating the paste, or gooping one or the other into their hair. The adult will spend more time restricting behavior than facilitating creativity, which is the purpose of making a collage.

One way to make collages appropriate for toddlers is to use Contact™ paper, sticky side out, and provide children with a number of safe objects to stick to it. A group of 12- to 24-month-olds at the Napa Valley College Child Development Center worked on a collage for several weeks as they continued to discover things to stick on the Contact™ paper left on a wall at their level. The continuing rearrangement of the collage elements showed how much more important the process is than the product at this age.

Some other activities that are easily modified are presented in Table 1.

How to Fit Programs to Toddlers

Adults who recognize the special needs of toddlers, such as sensorimotor learning and the development of autonomy, don't just tolerate this age group—they genuinely like toddlers. What do these knowledgeable adults do, then, to create a home or group setting that fits toddlers?

1. Structure the environment (rather than depending on adult rules). Put out only as many things as you can stand to pick up when they are dumped. One teacher suspended a bucket from the ceiling filled with things just for dumping. Make sure everything is touchable (and mouthable, depending on how young the children are). Provide space and equipment for large motor activity (climbing, jumping) inside as well as outside. Include plenty of softness (a mattress for jumping, pillows for wiggling on). Supply toys that can be used in many ways, such as blocks, as well as toys that are realistic (McLoyd, 1986). Remember, toddlers who are too excited, or bored, are apt to make themselves and everyone else unhappy, so keep activities and materials at a level they can handle. Watch the children's behavior to determine when the right amount of toys are available. Their needs may change from day to day.

2. Expect toddlers to test limits. That's their job, so the more the environment sets limits, the easier it will be for you. Again, judge whether the limits are just right, rather than too strict or too lax, by observing the children's behavior. If children insist on climbing on the table, for example, perhaps another climbing structure, or large pillows, or a crawl-through tunnel is needed. Are children randomly wandering without getting involved? Maybe more staff, or more attentive staff, are needed to be anchors for children as they reach out to new activities. Or possibly more variety and some new materials need to be offered. Rotate items—even after a week or two some will have new appeal.

Be consistent and firm about the limits you set, however. Otherwise children will be confused and will continue to test limits long after toddlerhood.

3. Stay out of power struggles. Toddlers can be very stubborn so it is a waste of energy to continually butt heads with them about enforcing limits. Use choices to avoid power struggles: "You can't walk around while you eat, but you can sit in either the blue chair or the red chair." Give toddlers frequent choices, but be sure what you offer are suitable alternatives. Usually a choice between two options is sufficient.

4. Direct behavior gently, but physically. Don't depend on words alone. Prevent dangerous behavior before it occurs—hold a threatening arm before it has a chance to hit. Lead a child by the hand back to the table to finish a snack. Don't let children get in trouble and then yell at them. If you find yourself saying "I knew that was going to happen," next time, don't predict—prevent it.

5. Expect lots of sensorimotor behavior. All furnishings, equipment, toys, and materials should be sturdy and safe enough to be dropped, mouthed, or climbed on. Dumping puzzles is as much fun as working them. The sound as the pieces hit the floor seems to be music to toddler ears. You can help children see the fun of putting puzzles back together, but don't expect to convince them right away that construction is more pleasurable than destruction.

6. Limit group activities to eating and maybe music or a short story time. Even then, form small groups, and expect children to leave to pursue something more exciting when they lose interest. Eventually they will want to be involved in larger and longer group activities, but toddlers are more individual doers than group listeners.

7. Share, wait, and use kind words to solve problems. But don't expect children to always follow the behavior you model. Toddlers cannot share until they first fully experience a sense of ownership. They need to see over and over again that they can trust that a favored item will not be taken away, or to find there are enough snacks for everyone so that grabbing and hoarding are not necessary. Have several of the same favorite toys.

Waiting is hard for adults and children—just remember the last time you had to wait in line! Organize routines so waiting does not consume most of the child's day. If a wait is unavoidable, keep children active with fingerplays or songs, for example, so they have something to do while they wait.

Even when toddlers lose control, adults need to maintain theirs by using words, rather than hitting or using harsh punishment, to solve problems. Choose words that respect children and support their needs, not words that ridicule or shame. For example, respond to a toileting accident with "Oh, Rosita, your clothes are all wet. They're probably uncomfortable for you, too. Let's find your dry clothes and then we'll wipe up the puddle," rather than "Look at the mess you made! Are we going to have to put you back in diapers?"

8. Be gentle and help children talk through problems. Fights and struggles are bound to occur, but children will learn to solve problems with each other sooner if you do what Gerber (1979) calls *sports announcing*—"I see how much you want that, Jason" rather than *refereeing*—"Amanda had it first, so give it to her." Avoid making arbitrary decisions for children, and instead help them search for constructive solutions.

9. Expect difficult behavior. Resistance to activities (wandering off in the middle of a song), rejection ("NO!"), and crying when they say goodbye to parents are all good behaviors—that's what toddlers should be doing. These behaviors show clearly that the children are in Erikson's stage of autonomy. Toddlers who are not developing well may appear depressed, have low self-esteem, seem to lack attachment to their families, or use one behavior in every situation. All toddlers won't exhibit difficult behaviors, but it is important to recognize such behaviors as normal and natural.

10. Define curriculum in realistic terms. An appropriate curriculum for toddlers is one that centers around

- self-care activities (such as eating, sleeping, toileting, and dressing),
- learning to cope with separation,
- making new attachments with children and adults, and
- free play in a safe and interesting environment.

All appropriate physical, cognitive, and socioemotional goals for toddlers fit easily into these activities.

11. Let toddlers be toddlers. Don't structure your curriculum around preparing toddlers for preschool by pushing them to act as if they are in a more advanced stage of development. When they have done very thoroughly what they need to do as 18-month-olds, or as 2-year-olds, or almost 3s, they will be ready to take on the tasks of a more advanced stage.

When we see toddlerhood as a special and distinct stage of development with its own set of tasks and behaviors, toddler's behavior becomes more understandable and manageable. Then we are not tempted to impose watered-down (or worse yet full-blown) preschool activities upon them. When we stop comparing toddlers with older children, and appreciate them for what they are, toddlers become very likable individuals. They will feel better about themselves because the adults who care for them respect them for what they should be—toddlers.

References

Erikson. E. H. (1963). *Childhood and society* (2nd ed.). New York: Norton.

Gerber. M. (1979). *Resources for infant educarers.* Los Angeles: Resources for Infant Educarers.

McLoyd. V. C. (1986). Scaffolds or shackles? The role of toys in preschool children's pretend play. In G. Fein & M. Rivkin (Eds.), *The young child at play: Reviews of research* (Vol. 4). Washington, DC: NAEYC.

Piaget. J. (1952). *The origins of intelligence in children* (M. Cook, Trans.). New York: International Universities Press.

Piaget, J. (1954). *The construction of reality in the child* (M. Cook, Trans.). New York: Basic.

Questions about Reading 11

1. Did you learn something about toddlers that you didn't know from reading this article?

2. How can you apply the information in this article to the 10 Principles in *Infants, Toddlers, and Caregivers*?

3. Some people think that the name "toddler" discriminates against children who are in that stage but because of a disability don't "toddle". Can you think of a better name for this stage that doesn't necessarily describe physical abilities?

Chapter 12

The Physical Environment

L ouis Torelli is an authority on infant-toddler environments, and with his partner, Charles Durret, is well known for creating beautiful environments that work. How much does this article correlate with the information in Chapter 12 in your text?

Reading 12

....

Creating a Landscape for Learning

Louis Torelli and Charles Durrett

A classroom learning environment should be highly functional, aesthetically attractive, age appropriate, child directed, and teacher supported. Incorporating a variety of levels as you redesign your classroom is one way to create such an environment. Through the use of platforms, lofts, recessed areas, low walls, and canopies placed along the periphery of the room, it is possible to sculpt your classroom into different activity areas.

The walls frame the activity areas while the center of the room remains fairly open, to allow for the circulation of children and adults as well as to provide flexible space that can change depending on the teacher's observations of the children's interests. Similar to a house that has a number of rooms, each with a different function, the multi-level environment provides places for various types of individual and small group play, such as reading, manipulatives, construction, dramatic play, and motor exploration.

Room Layout

Sculpting activity areas along the periphery

We've found that the most effective and efficient use of classrooms, which are typically short on space, is to carve out child-sized nooks for specific activity areas along the edge of the room. This layout makes supervision by the childcare provider easy, allowing children to engage in extended, individual and small group play, while the childcare provider supervises two or three of these activity areas simultaneously. Placing activity areas along the periphery of the room also allows children to play under natural sunlight next to the windows, and to look outside, maintaining a visual connection with the outdoor environment while indoors.

_____

Reprinted with permission from *www.spacesforchildren.com*

Your classroom can be sculpted into distinct activity areas through the use of low walls, or toy shelves acting as low walls, as well as by strategic placement of a Torelli/Durrett Infant or Toddler Loft (see Chapter Four, *Using Torelli/Durrett Equipment*). Low partitions allow the children to feel that they are in a discrete space, although they are easily supervised by the childcare provider. Though most activity areas will function best if designed with a specific activity in mind, some activity areas can be designed to be used more flexibly for group activities such as music and movement.

Incorporating a variety of levels

By varying the floor and ceiling levels within a classroom, even a relatively small classroom space can feel and function as several different environments. You can vary the floor levels using platforms and lofts and vary the ceiling heights by hanging canopies or creating childsized nooks. To determine where to use changes in level, first consider how you want each activity area to feel according to the specific activity you want to take place there. An intimate activity, such as reading, should feel private and removed from the excitement of activities such as water play, which should feel more open. A reading area, therefore, works well on a raised platform, while a water play area works best without a platform, leaving plenty of room to maneuver around it. Our Torelli/Durrett lofts create flexible activity areas on different levels. They create a special place for children to feel separate above the rest of the classroom, yet secure, in clear view of the childcare provider. At the same time, the space underneath the loft creates an intimate nook for a different kind of play, such as social drama.

Building a platform especially benefits those activities which work best contained within the designated area, such as blocks or small manipulatives. If a child is playing with blocks on a raised platform, the strong definition of the space naturally confines the block building to its own area instead of letting it spill into the activity area or circulation space next to it where it would be trampled on and knocked over.

Create a clear path of circulation

Both children and childcare providers benefit from making clear the distinction between areas to be used for activities and areas to be used for circulation. Children can play securely and for extended periods within an activity area, knowing that the building blocks they are stacking will not be trampled by other children or adults walking through their space. With adequate circulation, childcare providers can feel confident that they will not inadvertently step on a child. To differentiate activity areas, build low walls and platforms with equipment placed appropriately; or try changing the material of the floor, i.e., put linoleum in the circulation areas and carpet in the activity areas on either side.

Carefully planned storage

One goal of an effective classroom is to support the childcare provider in doing her job. She should be able to spend her time caring for children, not rushing across the room or even to another room trying to find what a child needs for an activity. For this reason, we recommend including plenty of storage that is easily accessible to each activity area in a classroom. An adequate and varied supply of children's play materials, stored on toy shelves, make taking out and putting away toys a child directed activity. We also suggest installing closed wall cabinets which only adults can access.

Maximizing Your Lighting

The lighting of a classroom must specifically support the developmental needs of infants and toddlers. Visual perception directly affects a child's ability to learn and interact with his environment. Lighting that is either too bright or too dim strains the eyes, harming visual development and leading to fatigue and crankiness. If the lighting does not work effectively with the environment to foster particular activities, both children and teachers will feel frustration. Poor lighting can negatively affect the general atmosphere of a classroom, but, when well thought out, lighting can harmoniously complement the intended activities of a space.

Improving artificial lighting

We recommend incandescent lighting rather than fluorescent because the quality of the light contributes to a child's visual development. Nearly every classroom we remodel is overlit initially by a flood of fluorescent light at the ceiling, which makes the space look and feel more like a hospital or an office than a place where children play. Incandescent lighting will make your classroom look and feel more like a home, which is especially important for children who spend up to ten hours a day in your care. Fluorescent lighting also often wastes energy by overlighting inappropriately. For example, a typical 700-square-foot classroom might have four rows of fluorescent lights, five lights per row, four forty-watt tubes per light. That calculates to 4.6 watts per square foot, which remains primarily at the ceiling level. However, two watts per square foot is sufficient if it is located where it is needed. Small children need appropriate lighting at the floor level where they spend the most time.

If your classroom is lit by fluorescent ceiling lights, we suggest as a minimum improvement replacing them with halogen track lights. Halogen track lights will offer warmer-toned light that you can direct in spots to light the floor or task area where children will be playing. Replacing with track lights is a fairly simple task, but an electrician can be helpful.

To bring light to the floor level, you can create "Pools" of light using pendant lights and track lights. Add indirect lighting using recessed lights or wall sconces. Dimmer switches: allow you to adjust the lighting according to the brightness needed at varying times of day and in support of various activities. For infants and toddlers, light should be provided at the floor level or the working surface, such as an easel or table.

People, especially children, are naturally drawn to light. Therefore, lighting should be used to attract them to certain activity areas, whether by using natural light or pools of incandescent light focused on a child-sized area. By creating pools of light at each activity area, a sense of containment and purpose is reinforced, giving children subtle boundaries for their activities.

Differentiating activity areas from circulation areas can also be accomplished with lighting, and can help to prevent children from being run into while they are playing.

Questions about Reading 12

1. Although this reading doesn't use the word curriculum, can you see how it relates to the ideas of curriculum in the other readings and in your textbook? Explain two places where environments and curriculum connect.

2. Why would you want to create a variety of levels in a room for infants and toddlers?

3. Torelli and Durrett give a large proportion of their chapter over to lighting. Why would lighting make a difference?

Chapter 13

The Social Environment

As stated in Chapter 13, positive identity development is more likely to come about when care and attention is taken to the social environment. One can see the physical environment, but the social environment is less tangible. Also, it isn't a matter of just knowing what is needed and providing it. No matter how dedicated those responsible are to creating a positive social environment, sometimes institutionalized policies and related practices make it difficult, if not impossible to make improvements. This article is about those social policies and reinforces what have been ongoing themes in your text throughout—primary caregiving, small groups, continuity of care, responsive curricula, and cultural continuity.

Reading 13

The Impact of Child Care Policies and Practices on Infant/Toddler Identity Formation

J. Ronald Lally

J. Ronald Lally, Ed.D., is director of WestEd's Center for Child and Family Studies, in Sausalito, California. He also directs the Program for Infant/Toddler Caregivers, a video-based training program. He is one of the founding members of Zero To Three.

An important distinction between infant/toddler care and preschool care has been ignored in all but the best programs and family child care homes. Preschoolers have formed a somewhat well-developed "working definition of self," with likes and dislikes, attitudes, and inclinations. Infants and toddlers are in the process of forming this preliminary sense of self. Part of what infants and toddlers get from caregivers are

Adapted from J. Ronald Lally, (1995) "The Impact of Child Care Policies and Practices on Infant/Toddler Identity Formation," *Young Children*, November, pp. 58-67.

perceptions of how people act at various times and in various situations (seen as how the infant should behave), how people act toward them and others (seen as how they and others should be treated), and how emotions are expressed (seen as how they should feel). The infant uses these impressions and often incorporates them into the self she becomes. This notion of the day-to-day influence of the caregiver on a child's evolving identity has often been overlooked in infant/toddler programs. More is happening than tender loving care and learning games—values and beliefs are being witnessed and incorporated.

Messages about appropriate and inappropriate infant and toddler behavior are influenced by child care policy. Some of the lessons that may become incorporated into the child's sense of self are:

- What to fear;
- Which of one's behaviors are seen as appropriate;
- How one's messages are received and acted upon;
- How successful one is at getting one's needs met by others;
- What emotions and intensity level of emotions one can safely display; and
- How interesting one is.

Culture is the fundamental building block of identity. Through cultural learning, children gain a feeling of belonging, a sense of personal history, and security in knowing who they are and where they come from. When infants are cared for by caregivers from a different cultural background, very often the child has his background either subtly or blatantly challenged. This is done often from the best of intentions. Different ways of doing things are often seen as strange. A child may become torn between how he is expected to behave at home—not to make such a mess—and how he is expected to behave in care—to touch and feel most anything.

The child care experience should be in harmony with the culture of the home. Therefore, caregivers should pay great attention to incorporating home practices into care. Patterns of care should give the child a sense of connection with the home and, more importantly, communicate that where she comes from is respected and appreciated. Staff should reflect the culture of the families served. These connections are important for the infant. Particularly if caregivers come from the same cultural background as the families and children served, the children will have an easy time incorporating their own cultures and values and beliefs into their emerging definition of self. It is particularly important that caregivers and families speak the same language.

With just the least bit of attention to issues of identity formation, caregivers can improve infant care outside the home. Having an orientation that acknowledges the caregiver's role in an infant's identity formation places the infant and the infant's work in proper perspective. It makes clear that those who care for infants and toddlers participate in the creation of a sense of self and that attention must be paid to this unique responsibility.

Questions about Reading 13

1. Lally's goal is for every infant and toddler to have a "solid sense of self." What does that concept mean to you?

2. Lally wrote this article in the mid-nineties. To your knowledge, have things changed? For example, he states that identity formation of infants and toddlers has been neglected by policy makers, teacher trainers, and others for two reasons. 1. Most infant toddler care programs are based on preschool models, which are inappropriate. 2. Infant/toddler care is not seen as a serious topic. What's your impression? How far has the field come since this article was written?

3. Lally says that caregivers influence infants' identity formation. The influence occurs when significant aspects of the way caregivers act are being perceived and interpreted by infants who automatically incorporate these perceptions and interpretations in their own definition of self. He gives examples of research to back up that statement. What is one such example?

Chapter 14

Adult Relations In Infant-Toddler Care and Education Programs

I nfants and toddlers always come in a context. That means that everything that has to do with their care and education also has to do with their families, so communication becomes very important! Although much of the communication between caregivers and families is "on the run" at the beginning and end of the day, at times there is the need to sit down and talk in a more formal way. What do you need to consider when planning and carrying out a conference with parents, other family members, or guardians when you don't share the same culture?

Reading 14

· ·

Cross Cultural Conferences

by Janet Gonzalez-Mena

Janet Gonzalez-Mena divides her time between teaching, writing, and family life. She taught for 15 years at Napa Valley College in California. The author of several books on early childhood, she also writes articles for early care and education publications.

Imagine you're waiting to meet with a parent who is of a culture that is different from yours. You know that there may be some cultural barriers to overcome, but you aren't sure what they are. The purpose of this article is to walk you through a parent conference pointing out where differences might lie.

There you are waiting. You wait and wait. The parent doesn't show up. Finally she arrives, but she doesn't even apologize for being late. Is this a misunderstanding, rudeness, lack of organization, or what?

It's quite possible that the two of you have a very different idea of what "late" means. There is enormous cultural variation in time concepts, and what may be "late" in one is "on time" in another. Some cultures tick off minutes, and each tick past the appointed time makes a person even tardier. Other folks may arrive several hours or even days after the appointed time and still consider themselves within the bounds of courtesy.

Then there's the greeting ritual. Do you shake hands or not? If yes, how? A firm handshake may mean you're a straightforward, confident, honest person—kind of like looking a person straight in the eye when you talk to her. A person who comes from that point of view may view a bare touching of the hands as a sign that the person is insecure, weak, or shady. However, in some cultures, a firm grip is rude and insensitive. And then there are people who never look you in the eye or touch during a greeting.

In many cultures, there are differences between how men greet each other, how women greet each other, and how greetings are conducted across the genders. How are you to know? You can't. You have to play it by ear and be sensitive to clues.

Are you a person who always wants to be on a first name basis to be warm and friendly while you're promoting equality? Oops. That may be a mistake. First names may feel uncomfortable or disrespectful to some parents. It's best to ask if you don't know. Asking "What do you want me to call you?" puts the ball in the parent's court.

Are you ready to close the magazine or turn the page and move on? Am I scaring you? There's so much to know—how can a person ever relate to someone of another culture and not make a million mistakes? That's an easy question to answer. You can't. You will make mistakes. So will the other person. You can't be expected to know everything there is to know about every other culture. Communicating across cultures is a learning experience. You have to approach it like that.

The best preparation for cross cultural encounters is to tune up your sensitivity. There's always more happening than there appears to be even in a simple encounter between two people of the same culture. The meaning of behavior and words is different for each person. Some of those differences are cultural and can be learned. Some are individual and can also be learned. Think of yourself as a lifetime learner and it won't be so overwhelming.

Finally, you've gotten through the greetings and are ready to deal with the business of the conference. But are you? Perhaps the parent is used to some casual chitchat before getting down to business. Have you planned time for this? For a person who operates on a tight schedule and wants to get down to business right away, idle conversation can be frustrating. But if you perceive that a little socializing is in order, it might be worth it to devote a few minutes anyway just to set the tone for the conference.

Okay, you're finally ready to talk about whatever the subject of this conference is. Don't use jargon. Prepare ahead of time by translating all the professional terms into plain English. Otherwise you will more than likely lose the parent. Even worse, you'll create a power imbalance. When professionals explain things in ways that aren't easy to understand, they put themselves in a lofty position. This use of jargon can even be perceived as "peacocking" by some parents—that is, spreading out a glorious tail to wow or perhaps woo the onlooker.

Power stances in exchanges between parents and professionals are a big issue and one you should sort out for yourself. When you're personally involved in a game of one-up-manship with parents, who usually wins? How dedicated are you to sharing power? How knowledgeable are you about how to do it? Power plays get in the way of true communication, and, after all, you're aiming for an honest exchange, aren't you?

Then there is the issue of cultural perspectives. How closely do the parent's ideas about what's good for children match yours? The image the parent has of a child may be diametrically opposed to the program's image. It's easy to criticize a parent who "babies" her child, or overprotects him, for example. But do you really understand her priorities? The program goals may be independence and individuality, while the parent sees those goals as getting in the way of keeping the child firmly connected to his family. Another example: you may be promoting self-esteem, while the parent sees pride in one's accomplishments as the greatest sin of all.

Whew! You may be about to close the magazine again. Don't give up. The solution is to put yourself in the parent's shoes and try to feel what it would be like to walk in them. Use your best listening skills—the ones you use for children who try to communicate with you but have problems.

As soon as you discover that instead of listening you are trying to form your own response, stop yourself. This isn't easy to do. If you listen to an average conversation between two people, you will discover that the talk often moves back and forth between one speaker's agenda and the other's with only a thread of connection between the two.

Give up your concern with your agenda and really listen to the parent—not only the words, but the feelings behind them. Listen until the person stops talking. Don't interrupt. When it's your turn, instead of arguing, educating, or responding from your own perspective, try to state the perspective of the other person. Put the gist or spirit of what you heard into words by making a statement about the other person's feelings, experiences, perceptions, beliefs, or concepts. See if you can get at the deeper message.

Most people do little of this kind of listening and responding. In a conversation where there is disagreement, most people constantly push forward their own point of view.

Listening skills can be learned. And best of all is the feedback you get when you've received the message someone was trying to send. It's like practicing with a basketball; you know when you've made a basket. You know you've opened up communication because the ball slides through the hoop and the conversation continues.

Communicating in a cross cultural situation can be rewarding. Mistakes are usually forgiven once the parent sees that you are trying hard to meet her on a level playing field.

Imagine that you are watching the door close after a successful conference. Imagine that after the last goodbye you sit back satisfied that you and the parent have experienced good communication. It was worth the struggle; it was worth risking mistakes. You both learned something. Can you ask more than that?

Questions about Reading 14

1. What experiences have you had with people who had a different idea of what "on time" meant from your idea?

2. What do you know about greeting people from cultures different from your own?

3. Do you automatically call someone by his or her first name? If yes, why? If no, why not?

Overarching Themes

Readings on Health and Safety

Creating a sense of security for infants, toddlers, and their families is a primary concern. The following articles deal with risk factors for infants while sleeping, caring for a child whose development is affected by a health problem, and promoting breast feeding in child care settings.

Read what Susan Aronson has to say about infants sleeping safely in child care settings. Think about what you know and have heard about sleeping positions for infants.

Reading 15

···

Sudden Infant Death Syndrome

Ask Dr. Sue your health and safety questions

by Susan S. Aronson, MD

Preventable SIDS Deaths Occur in Child Care

Too many infants are dying in child care from Sudden Infant Death Syndrome (SIDS)—in part because child care providers still put babies to sleep on their tummies. This startling finding was reported in the July 1997 issue of *Pediatrics*. In the article, the researchers summarized their telephone survey of how child care centers put infants to sleep in Washington, DC, and two nearby counties. They obtained responses from 131 of 137 licensed centers, or 96% of licensed centers that care for infants in the metropolitan area.

Publicity about the prevention of SIDS when infants sleep on their backs has been associated with remarkable reduction in tummy positioning for infants and a precipitous drop in SIDS deaths. In 1992, over 70% of US parents put their infants to sleep on their tummies. By 1995, only 30% of parents put their infants to sleep prone.

However, in 1996, half of child care centers in the Washington metropolitan area reported that they did not know the current national recommendation that all infants be put to sleep on their backs. Roughly the same proportion reported that they put at least some infants to sleep on their tummies. In 20% of the centers, the respondents said that all infants were put to sleep in this dangerous position.

This problem is not limited to the nation's capital. Two states have data showing that a disproportionately high percentage of SIDS deaths occur in child care facilities. The Minnesota SIDS Center reports that the percentage of SIDS deaths in organized child care may be as high as 35.4%. In California, over 40% of SIDS deaths occur in child care. These rates of SIDS deaths in child care are higher than expected. According to the US Census Bureau, only 17% of infants in the United States were in child care centers (8%) and family child care homes (9%) in 1993.

In the Washington study, even among those centers that reported they knew about the risk of tummy positioning for sleep, less than half practiced safe positioning. These centers said their reasons for using the dangerous tummy-sleeping position included child comfort, instructions from the child's parents, a mistaken belief that back sleeping is less important after three months of age, and the common misperception that children are more likely to choke if they sleep on their backs.

Reprinted with permission from *Child Care Information Exchange* PO Box 3249, Redmond, WA 98073, (800) 221-2864. *www.ChildCareExchange.com*

SIDS is a devastating occurrence in a child care facility. The death of a child is a loss of enormous significance to the child's family, the staff, and the community. The legal and financial cost to the program can be ruinous. When at least half of SIDS deaths can be prevented by putting infants to sleep on their backs, why would child care providers ever do anything else?

. . . .

Questions about Reading 15

1. What can be done to cut down the risk factors of infants dying of Sudden Infant Death Syndrome or SIDS, (also called crib death) in child care?

2. What is your experience in putting babies to sleep?

3. What would you do about babies who appear to be more comfortable when put to sleep on their stomachs?

A ccording to Cynthia Huffman, caregivers face some unique challenges when a child with special needs enrolls, including developing health care and emergency plans and determining appropriate adaptations to activities and the environment. Infants and toddlers are most vulnerable to the effects of hospitalization or a health care crisis.

Reading 16

· ·

Supporting the Development of Infants and Toddlers with Special Health Needs

by Cynthia Huffman, MS, CCLS*
Edited by Susan S. Aronson MD, FAAP

Dr. Sue Aronson, MD, FAAP, is clinical professor of pediatrics at the University of Pennsylvania and a pediatrician in Philadelphia, Pennsylvania.

Cynthia Huffman is a trainer for The National Lekotek Center in their Inclusion Through Play project, which assists teachers in including children with disabilities in early childhood settings. She was formerly a child life specialist at Childrens Hospital Los Angeles and conducts professional development workshops that focus on helping young children and their families cope with special health care needs, loss, and grief. She earned her master's degree from the Infant/Parent Development and Early Intervention Program at Bank Street College of Education.

At some time in their careers, almost all child care workers will care for a child whose development is affected by a special health problem. Recent medical advances, current trends in managed care, increased demand for child care, and legislatively mandated inclusion have increased the number of children with chronic illness and special health needs in child care facilities. Although varying definitions yield different results, most estimates indicate that between 18% and 30% of children under 18 in the United States are affected by chronic developmental, behavioral, and physical conditions (USHHS, 1996). Here's what we do know:

- The emotional, physical, and intellectual experiences of a child's first three years are vital, laying the foundation for that child's development in the future.

Reprinted with permission from *Child Care Information Exchange*, PO Box 3249, Redmond, WA 98073, (800) 221-2864
www.ChildCareExchange.com

*Certified Child Life Specialist—Child Life is a profession focusing on the emotional and developmental needs of children in the context of health care. A Child Life Specialist must achieve specific educational standards, which include earning a minimum of a baccalaureate degree in child life, psychology, child development, human and family studies, or another closely related field. For certification, a Child Life Specialist must complete a 480-hour internship in a child life program, under the direct supervision of a Certified Child Life Specialist followed by a comprehensive, written examination given by the Child Life Council. Requirements to maintain certification include professional development hours, which can include: lectures, college courses, and seminars relating to direct and indirect patient care, as well as required re-testing with the Child Life Council at regular intervals.

- Approximately 40% of children four years and younger have at least one hospital visit each year (National Health Care Survey, 1999). Every young child should have regularly scheduled well-child (check-up) visits to a doctor where the presence of acute and chronic health problems should be detected and managed as early in the child's life as possible.
- Research repeatedly indicates that older infants and toddlers (six months to three years) are the most vulnerable to the effects of hospitalization or a health care crisis (Vernon, Foley, Sipowicz, & Schulman, 1965).
- Medical advances and current trends in managed care have resulted in shorter hospital stays for children. Often, these hospitalizations are intense and associated with significant stress. After a hospitalization, children may show behavior problems, sleep problems, or regressions in previously learned developmental skills at home and in their child care programs.

Caregivers face some unique challenges when a child with special needs enrolls or returns to their care. In addition to obtaining accurate current information, developing health care and emergency plans, and determining appropriate adaptations to activities and the environment, caregivers must be prepared to provide immediate and sensitive support for emotional and developmental needs of these children.

The role of the child life professional developed in response to increasing evidence that illness, chronic conditions, and hospitalizations can disrupt the development of children and effective family functioning. Research consistently demonstrates that the negative impact of illness and hospitalization can be modified by specific interventions (Thompson, 1985). While other members of the health care team generally focus on medical issues, child life specialists focus on supporting the child's strengths to minimize stress and anxiety to promote optimal growth and development.

As advocates for children and their families, child life professionals provide opportunities for children to learn, express themselves, and gain a sense of mastery. In addition they facilitate socialization and family involvement in the care of their hospitalized child. By working with the child life specialist who can advise about how to support children with hospitalization stress, caregivers can combine their knowledge of child development with child life theory and practice, to provide appropriate support to children with special health needs.

Impact of Chronic Illness and Hospitalization

Children and adults experience hospitalization as a stress. Coping improves with increased experiences with hospital and medical environments and with opportunities to verbalize what the hospital experiences mean. Many adults relive and retell friends and relatives about hospital experiences repeatedly as they recover. The stress of a medical experience is particularly difficult for infants and toddlers to manage. They cannot work through the experience by talking about it.

For infants: One of the primary tasks for the child in the first year of life is to develop trust that basic needs will be met by the adults who care for them. For infants, illness can disrupt the normal routines and rhythms that allow them to feel safe and secure. They may have received too much stimulation and inconsistent nurturing. A baby who has had a serious illness may have limited capacity to receive proper nutrition and to explore, both of which may disrupt physical, social, and cognitive development. Furthermore, the distressing impact of illness may cause the baby's parents to withdraw emotionally. When parents are emotionally withdrawn or exhausted, the infant may be unable to develop a secure attachment to them.

During hospitalization, a baby's sensory experiences will be very different from those at home. The sights, sounds, and smells of a hospital are often overwhelming for infants. Confined mostly to a hospital crib, babies will have few opportunities to learn by exploring the world around them. In the hospital, social interactions are often intrusive and abrupt. Health care teams are on constantly rotating shifts. In these circumstances it may be very difficult for a young infant to develop or maintain trust and to form normal attachments.

For toddlers: Illness and hospitalization threaten a toddler's developing autonomy. Some fight to maintain control and others relinquish all control. The symptoms of illness may restrict activities that provide the practice to master typical tasks of toddlerhood such as motor, language, and self-help skills. Young children do not understand illness. Their magical and egocentric thinking may lead them to believe they caused their own illness or that their illness is punishment for bad behavior.

During hospitalization, separation from parents is the greatest concern, even for a toddler who has learned to cope with routine separations. Such separation may be viewed as abandonment, a sign of lost love, or as punishment. Hospitals may provide few opportunities for normal socialization and success in accomplishing simple tasks. With limited opportunities to develop self-confidence, hospitalized toddlers may become cautious about pursuing new experiences and may require more adult reassurance.

Unfamiliar surroundings and intrusive procedures by strangers are frightening for toddlers. Hospitalized toddlers may show increased intensity in their reactions and behavioral responses to stress as well as changes in their daily habits such as eating, toileting, and sleeping. Regression in any or all areas of development may occur. Such regression may be intensified by physical and emotional disruptions in parent support.

Helping Infants and Toddlers Cope

A young child with special health needs is first and foremost a child. As with all children, caring requires an ongoing process of evaluating needs, planning and carrying out a course of action, evaluating results, re-evaluating needs, and revising the course of action as necessary. The strategies that facilitate growth and development for all children are applicable, but some children may need extra help. Some may require more time to practice new tasks as well as some adaptation of the environment, activities, or materials.

The sequence of developmental milestones is the same for all children—with or without chronic illness—but illness and its resulting symptoms may slow the rate of development. Some children with chronic illness or those who have had frequent or prolonged hospitalizations may not have successfully mastered the developmental tasks of infancy. You may need to help an 18-month-old develop trust and feel secure or help a three-year-old child learn to feed himself.

After an infant or toddler has experienced a health crisis or hospitalization, caregivers should be prepared for the need to reestablish trust—no matter how strong the prior relationship. Soothe, comfort, and respond immediately to an infant's expressions of need or discomfort. Make an extra effort to maintain schedules that match the baby's rhythms. Be very alert to body language that may indicate that the child is ready for interaction. Within limits determined by medical issues, provide appropriate stimulation and freedom for an infant to explore and master new experiences.

Toddlers may need frequent confirmation that they are loved and cared for by trusted adults. Reassure them that the illness or hospitalization is not their fault and that it is not punishment for bad behavior. Maintain schedules for consistency while providing choices that allow the toddler as much control over the environment as possible. Encourage mastery of self-help skills and socialization, but be patient. The child needs time to regain previously mastered skills. Support any reliance the child has on security objects and other successful self-coping strategies. Encourage independence but remember all children need age-appropriate discipline and limits.

Like all toddlers, those with special health needs will struggle to sort out and express their emotions. A limited vocabulary may prevent a young child from describing different emotions. Some may have the language skills but may not be willing to talk about feelings, especially if the child is afraid those feelings will be considered unacceptable. Encourage and validate all expressions of emotions.

While you may see regression in some areas of development, you may also see disproportionate maturity in other areas as a result of the grown-up knowledge and experience that illness and treatment can bring. So while caregivers should support developmentally appropriate behavior, they should also acknowledge children who show unexpected maturity when they try to express themselves and cope with their world.

Be alert in your observations. All children with chronic illness will not behave a certain way. Children often behave according to adult expectations. When the illness has been significant, there is a tendency to focus on medical issues and any resulting developmental delays. Such a focus may make it difficult to see a child's strengths, which are the basis for continued growth. If problems do occur, remember that they may represent combinations of factors and not entirely result from the illness.

Play

As in all of early childhood education, the heart of child life is providing play experiences. Play is the way children progress. It is critical to child development. Play promotes progress toward developmental milestones. It is the means through which children learn, socialize, and express feelings.

Play is a way for young children to resolve difficult events they have experienced. Appropriately safe physical play such as banging, pounding, and throwing activities provides a release of the energy, anger, and frustration that illness and hospitalization can generate. Music and movement also offer opportunities for infants and toddlers to express emotions and release energy. In addition to developmentally supportive play for all children in their care, caregivers should facilitate medical play, which focuses on emotional issues related to health care. Recently hospitalized toddlers will often act out separation anxiety or medical procedures in dramatic play, which may reveal their fears about what happened or might happen next. You may be able to facilitate this play by taking on the role of the toddler allowing the child to feel in control by playing the grown up.

Frightened and angry about all the injections they received, toddlers may run around pretending to give shots to others as they attempt to sort out their feelings about this medical experience. If it hurts or frightens others, encourage the expression of the feelings but direct the actions to inanimate objects like dolls or animal figures. Try to positively reinforce effective coping strategies and whenever safely possible, let the child choose from alternative strategies. As always you should keep the child's family advised of any concerns that are revealed through play.

You can help toddlers explore medical equipment and use it to express themselves in art. Using materials like tongue depressors, specimen cups, and paper medicine cups in non-threatening art activities allows children to become more familiar with these materials, reducing their fear of them. These activities can also help toddlers to identify experiences and express their feelings about them.

Helpful Materials to Have in Your Child Care Facility

A variety of materials can help young children cope with illness and health care experiences. Most are available in educational supply catalogues. They should be readily accessible so that you can encourage their use on an ongoing basis, not just when a crisis arises.

- Books that include children with all kinds of differences, including illness and disabilities. The books should include both those where the difference is the focus of the story, and those where the difference is not relevant to the narrative. Diversity should be presented as a natural part of the world.
- Books that explore going to the doctor, dentist, hospital, clinic, or eye doctor.
- Wall pictures that reflect these experiences for a diversity of children and families.
- Play materials that reflect people with special needs such as eyeglasses without lenses, dolls with walkers, and wheelchairs for dolls.
- Medical clothing in the dress-up corner, e.g., child-size scrubs, surgical masks, and disposable hair cover. (Any headgear should be used for one child and then discarded to prevent transmission of lice from one child to another.)

- Medical materials like bandages, cloth (choke-safe) adhesive strips, specimen cups, paper medicine cups, tongue depressors, alcohol wipes, X-ray films. Both real and toy medical instruments such as a stethoscope, an otoscope, a blood pressure cuff, and syringes without needles.

Helping Families Cope

Health care crises present an important time for families to believe they can trust you. They need a place to vent feelings and fears without being judged. They will need your input on how their child is coping. Be careful to avoid adding to any guilt that they may already be feeling.

Sometimes it's hard for parents to talk with their children about things that might upset them. Illness, pain, and death are so difficult for adults to deal with that they often want to shelter the innocent from the anxiety they can produce. We know from experience, however, that helping young children understand what to expect and what they have observed can make visits to the doctor, a health care crisis, or hospitalization much easier for them. If you know a child in your care will require hospitalization, encourage the family to make use of any child life services available at their hospital. If there are none, help them prepare by providing other resources. In addition to the materials for use in your classroom, many major hospitals offer helpful information on their websites.

If the child's health care team has not prepared the family for potential behavior changes, especially after crisis or hospitalization, help them understand what is happening. Explain that although all children do not exhibit these behavior changes, those that they are witnessing are fairly typical. Parents often worry that regressions may be permanent. If the child's medical team has not indicated a lasting or permanent disability, help parents understand that with a little extra patience, attention, and reassurance, their child will return to previously exhibited skills.

Quality child care encourages family participation in the program, but family involvement is especially important when a child has special health needs. Not only will this coordinate care for the child at home and in the program, it will help the child feel safe and secure, and will allow child care staff to look for opportunities to renew the family's confidence in their own abilities as caregivers.

Many parents are understandably overprotective after a diagnosis or medical crisis. Sensitive supportive care for their child by the child care staff may help ease their fears. Be a role model for parents by cautiously allowing the child to return to normal activities. Show them how to accept the child's limits and, while protecting the child from danger and frustration, allow opportunities for growth and development.

Remember that both the children in your care and their families may need help from other professionals. Encourage them to get the support and services they need. Work with the child's pediatrician and other medical professionals to facilitate referrals to competent resources for family support in the community.

For more information:

The Child Life Council
11820 Parklawn Drive, #202
Rockville, Maryland 20852-2529
Phone: (301) 881-7090
www.childlife.org.

References

Hart, K, Mather, P. L., Slack, J. E, & Powell. M. A. (1992). *Therapeutic Play Activities for Hospitalized Children.* St. Louis: Mosby-Year Book, Inc.
National Center for Health Statistics, National Health Care Survey, 1999.

Thompson, K H. (1985). *Psychosocial research on pediatric hospitalization and health care—A review of the literature*. Springfield, IL. Charles C. Thomas.

Trends in the Well-Being of America's Children and Youth: 1996 USHIHS, Office of the Assistant Secretary for Planning and Evaluation.

Vernon, D. T. A., Foley, J. M., Sipowicz, & Schulman, J. L. (1965). *The psychological responses of children to hospitalization and illness*. Springfield, IL: Charles C. Thomas.

Questions about Reading 16

The negative impact of illness and hospitalization can be modified by specific interventions. The following questions help you explore some specific ways to help infants, toddlers and their families cope with possible difficult situations.

1. Infants may need help with trust issues. What are some specific ways caregivers can help them establish or reestablish trust?

2. Toddlers may need help with trust issues and also issues around autonomy. What are some ways that caregivers can respond to their special needs?

3. How can *play* help children resolve difficult events they have experienced and relieve stress?

4. What are two things caregivers can do to help parents work through their infant's or toddler's hospitalization and/or illness?

Breastmilk provides the ideal nutrition for babies and has many health benefits, so promoting breastfeeding in child care is important. Read the next article to see if you agree.

Reading 17

....

Breastfeeding Promotion in Child Care

by Laura Dutil Aird

Laura Dutil Aird, MS, a former child care center director, is the director for the Division of Community Health Services at the American Academy of Pediatrics in Elk Grove Village, Illinois.

Twenty years ago, I was a recent college graduate who had just opened up a new child care center in Libertyville, Illinois. A parent who enrolled her daughter in our infant room asked if she could come to the center on her lunch hour to breastfeed. It didn't occur to me that I was promoting the health of that infant and her mother, strengthening the bond between them, or easing the mother's transition back to work—I was simply accommodating a parental request. Since then, public awareness about breastfeeding has increased, and most of us recognize that breastfeeding is widely recommended for virtually all infants because of its numerous advantages over alternative feedings.

What We Know

Research shows that human milk or breastmilk, with its unique mixture of fatty acids, lactose, amino acids, vitamins, minerals, enzymes, and other components necessary for digestion, brain development, and growth, provides the most natural and beneficial first food. Breastmilk both nourishes babies and protects them from getting sick.

Exclusive breastfeeding is ideal nutrition and sufficient to support the optimal growth and development of infants until they are approximately six months old. Continued breastfeeding is recommended throughout the baby's first year and thereafter as long as is mutually desired.

Breastfeeding benefits for the infant include reduction of the infectious disease risks that are greater in group child care including diarrhea, lower respiratory illness, otitis media, bacteremia, bacterial meningitis, botulism, urinary tract infections, necrotizing enterocolitus, SIDS, insulin dependent diabetes, lymphoma, allergic disease, ulcerative colitus, and other chronic digestive diseases. Breastfeeding also is associated with enhanced cognitive development.

There are also a number of studies that indicate possible health benefits for mothers. Breastfeeding helps mothers to recover more rapidly after delivery including an earlier return to their prepregnant weight.

Reprinted with permission from *Child Care Information Exchange*, PO Box 3249, Redmond, WA 98073, (800) 221-2864
www.ChildCareExchange.com

Breastfeeding also helps to reduce the risk of ovarian cancer, premenopausal breast cancer, and hip fractures in the postmenopausal period.

Breastfeeding is practical because it costs less than formula; there is less trash and pollution because there are fewer cans, bottles, and nipples to wash or throw away; and it leads to healthier people.

Breastfeeding helps babies and mothers develop a special closeness and helps mothers feel good about child care because they can continue to breastfeed.

Trends

Although breastfeeding is endorsed in the United States as the ideal infant feeding method and rates have increased over the past two decades, initiation rates are still behind national goals and generally are lower in poorer socioeconomic groups.

In 2000, 68% of mothers initiated breastfeeding and 31% continued to breastfeed at six months. Tremendous disparities exist for race and ethnicity, education level, employment, age, and Special Supplemental Nutrition Program for Women, Infants, and Children (WIC) eligibility. However, mothers' attitudes often are a stronger predictor of breastfeeding than sociodemographics. Prior breastfeeding experience, the support of close family and friends, and whether breastfeeding was portrayed as the norm when they were growing up all influence a mother's decision to breastfeed.

Breastfeeding and the Workplace

Surveys show that although breastfeeding is on the rise and the number of women in the workplace is increasing, most employed women do not concurrently breastfeed. The high participation rate in the workforce by young women and their early return to work after delivery conflicts with current breastfeeding recommendations. Mothers indicate several barriers to breastfeeding and working including scheduling difficulties, finding quality child care, negative reactions of colleagues, and the absence of adequate family and societal support. Continued breastfeeding after return to work is important, but it presents a challenge that demands societal support, legislative protection, and innovative solutions.

Companies are finding that it pays to help employed women reach their breastfeeding goals—doing so results in fewer infant illnesses, less absenteeism, more satisfied and loyal employees, and lower retraining costs. Mothers who continue to breastfeed after returning to work can appreciate the maternal health benefits of nursing, feel more connected to their baby, and enjoy continued opportunities to nurse when they are together. When asked, mothers stated that continuing to breastfeed after returning to work had positive effects on their self-image and their relationship with the infant's father. Mothers also report several factors that ease the transition into the workplace, including child care by a trusted individual, on-site child care, support in the workplace, access to support groups, successful role models, family support, and a good diet.

Although exclusive breastfeeding for the first six months is ideal, breastfeeding does not have to be an all-or-nothing experience. Some working mothers have mentioned that using formula to supplement breastfeeding as well as increasing breastfeeding at night and on weekends helped them in their efforts to continue breastfeeding.

How Early Childhood and Child Care Programs Can Support Breastfeeding

Except in the presence of rare genetic diseases, the obvious advantage of human milk over any formula should lead to vigorous efforts by child care providers to promote and sustain breastfeeding for mothers who desire to nurse their babies whenever they can and to pump and supply their milk to the child care facility when direct feeding from the breast is not possible. Even if infants receive formula during the child care day, any amount of breastfeeding or drinking of expressed human milk from their mothers is beneficial.

The recently revised national health and safety standards, called *Caring for Our Children*, offers national guidelines for out-of-home child care programs. The standards require that child care facilities encourage and support breastfeeding as well as have a designated place set aside for breastfeeding mothers who want to come during work to breastfeed. Also, the standards indicate what must be done if the milk of one child's mother is inadvertently fed to someone else's child.

> *Caring for Our Children: the national health and safety performance standards, guidelines for out-of-home child care,* 2002 is available on the Internet at www.nrc.uchsc.edu and in hard copy from the American Academy of Pediatrics, (800) 227-1770, Publications Department.

Child care providers and administrators can tailor the level of their involvement depending on their interests and comfort level. They can:

- Support mothers in their decision to continue breastfeeding and talk about why breastfeeding is so good for babies.
- Tell parents that they are happy to care for breastfed babies and are willing to feed them expressed breastmilk.
- Display "Breastfed Babies Are Welcome Here!" signs and offer educational materials for parents that include accurate and practical information.
- Welcome breastfeeding moms who come during the day, and offer a private, comfortable place for them to nurse.
- Listen empathically and help mothers to articulate their breastfeeding goals.
- Develop a plan in concert with the parents so that the baby can be fed on demand but, whenever possible, can be breastfed by the mother.
- Include fathers and other supportive relatives or partners in decisions related to the baby's care, and encourage them to feel good about the role they play in supporting continued breastfeeding.
- Explain to preschool and school-age children that breastfeeding is the normal and preferred way to feed babies, and emphasize that breastfeeding contributes to a child's and mother's well-being.
- Bring staff together to determine the best practices for your program.
- Partner with others to identify/utilize community resources and promote systems of community support.

Child care providers and parents should be aware of and implement safe breastmilk storage and handling procedures.

Personal Experience

One issue to consider is how personal experience affects our ability to do what's best for children and their families. Perhaps you did not choose to breastfeed your child or may have wanted to breastfeed but were unable to do so. Or you might not be comfortable talking about "breasts" or may see them only as a private body part that is sexual in nature. By thinking about your own experiences and considering your comfort level with breastfeeding, you can determine how best to support the children and parents you see on a day-to-day basis.

All parents want to do what is best for their baby. With your support, parents will feel comfortable articulating their breastfeeding goals—and together you can develop a plan that meets everyone's needs.

Resources

American Academy of Pediatrics, Work Group on Breastfeeding (1997). Breastfeeding and the use of human milk. *Pediatrics, 100* (6): 1035–1039.

American Academy of Pediatrics (2002). *Caring for our children, national health and safety performance standards: Guidelines for out-of-home child care programs.* Elk Grove Village, IL: American Academy of Pediatrics/American Public Health Association/National Resource Center for Health and Safety in Child Care.

Meek, J. Y. (2001). Breastfeeding in the Workplace. *Pediatric Clinics* of *North America, 48:* 461–474.

Neifert, M. (2000). *Supporting breastfeeding mothers as they return to work.* Elk Grove Village, IL: American Academy of Pediatrics.

United States Breastfeeding Committee (2001). *Breastfeeding in the United States: A national agenda.* Rockville, MD: US Department of Health and Human Services, Health Resources and Services Administration, Maternal and Child Health Bureau.

US Department of Health and Human Services *(2000). HHS Blueprint for Action on Breastfeeding.* Washington, DC: US Department for Health and Human Services, Office on Women's Health.

Questions about Reading 17

1. Do you have any feelings about breastfeeding in general or specifically about supporting breastfeeding in infant-toddler programs?

2. If your feelings lead you to be hesitant about using the suggestions in the article, what can you do about those feelings?

3. The article lists seven things to do to support breastfeeding in child care. Explain four of them.

Readings on Culture
and Families

C aregiving routines give cultural messages, even if the caregiver doing them is unaware of any cultural implications. Read the following article to learn more about this subject as it relates to feeding routines. Pay attention to any feelings that arise as you read the five observations on feeding babies that open the article.

Reading 18

....

Cultural Dimensions of Feeding Relationships

by Carol Brunson Phillips and Renatta M. Cooper

Carol Brunson Phillips, of the Council for Early Childhood Professional Recognition

Renatta M. Cooper of the Pacific Oaks College and Children's School

My husband and I prepare the food that our children (Chloe, 3 years; John, 5 months) get. We cook it ourselves, using as little processed foods as possible. We put food out that we feel is balanced, and Yolanda feeds them when we are not here. It's pretty clear what they can have, and we don't get uptight about the amount they eat on a day-to-day basis. My pediatrician said not to be uptight about what they eat—they will eat a balanced diet, but may not eat a balanced meal . . .

   (When I was a child) the food was laid out in traditional Chinese style, and we used chop sticks and spoons. Meals were very formal, no one was allowed to touch anything until everyone was seated. It was the time of day when we all connected . . .

   . . . I don't know any woman who doesn't breastfeed . . .

—Joy Lee*, Chinese American, professional, age 39

One of my nipples wouldn't come out, and the baby just went to sleep when I was trying to feed her. The nurse suggested that I just give her formula, and my Mom said that it would be okay too, so I did. It makes it easier for other people to feed her . . .

   . . . She's been receiving solids since she was two months old. I just wanted to see if she would sleep better. The doctor said she didn't need any solids for a year, but my Mom and I decided that if we gave her cereal at night, that she would sleep through the night . . . I want to be the one to introduce new foods to her so I can see what she likes and dislikes.

—Michelle Scott, African American,
clerical worker, age 20

I was always inclined toward self feeding . . . I'd rather clean up the mess than have a battle over eating. I've seen other parents who feed their children, and they're still sitting next to

Reprinted with permission from *Zero to Three*, www.zerotothree.org

*Names of respondents and their families have been changed

them when they're five—making sure that they eat. I've never wanted that. To be relaxed about meals was natural for me . . .

When others feed my kids, it's important that they feel in charge. I want them to feel comfortable. I hire people that I'm comfortable with, and it's okay if their style is different . . .

—Linda Levy, European American (Jewish),
upper-middle-class mother at home, age 36

At first, spilling food worried me a lot (because of the mess). I just wasn't raised that way.

—Alex Levy, European American (Jewish),
entrepreneur, age 41

It works best to hire staff who have children of their own, it gives them something to draw on. Those people with 12 early childhood credits and no practical experience don't have the patience that it takes to work with these children day in and day out . . . Some of the staff put cereal in these babies' bottles. I know that they shouldn't do it—but it gets frustrating feeding these kids. Sometimes you just want to make sure that they've had enough.

—Clara Davis, African American, site director of a group
home for infants and toddlers who have been affected by their mothers' drug use, age 50+

These observations on feeding babies and young children were made by parents and caregivers of infants and toddlers, interviewed in California early in 1992. Asked to comment on cultural dimensions of the feeding relationship for this issue of *Zero to Three*, we thought about aspects of culture that play a significant role in how children are fed. As we talked to parents as a way to begin our thinking, we were reminded that given the intricate combinations of race, ethnicity, educational level, and class that contribute to our country's diversity, isolating culture is a complex endeavor.

As students of the role of culture in child development, we realized that the parents we talked to were indeed revealing cultural influences from their own families. Yet these parents and caregivers were also revealing their response to American "child development" traditions. In this tradition, professional credentials confer authority (It is permissible for a parent to be relaxed about a toddler's food intake if the pediatrician tells her "not to be uptight.") Even professionals with relatively low status in the larger world, such as nursing assistants and child care providers, have tremendous power in early feeding relationships: They facilitate breastfeeding, or don't; they elicit and accommodate individual parents' feeding preferences or create a culture of group care; they follow parent/employers' instructions to the letter or develop their own unique feeding relationship with the baby in their care.

At the same time, we have long been aware that "child development tradition" itself is full of pervasive ethnocentrism, exhibited in the professional literature as well as among practitioners. Much of what we know as "child development" is the product of a predominantly North American/European scientific endeavor and tradition, resulting in a narrow database (Nugent et al., 1989). Although there is a growing awareness that empirical findings reported in the literature cannot be generalized to most of the world's children today, we frequently find descriptions of children that nonetheless make assumptions about "normal development" from a Eurocentric perspective. And assumptions about "normal development" quickly become, of course, the foundation for ideas about what is "developmentally appropriate" practice.

Take the issue of self feeding among infants and toddlers, for example. The experts (Leach, Spock) tell us that it is important to encourage babies to take part in the feeding process, even though a mess results. Child care providers who are sensitive to the demands on families may not urge parents to allow messy self feeding attempts at home. But true to the tradition of "child development," these professional caregivers will make sure that there is time for children to learn self-feeding skills in the child care setting. The adults will clean up the mess. The children will move toward sturdy independence.

But what if early independence turns out not to be valued by a family? Consuelo Aquino (in Clark, 1981, cited in Mangione, 1995) writes:

(In my culture) the baby is considered a very precious thing. As the baby grows he is watched closely with loving concern. Expectations are kept below the child's potential . . . all problems are met indirectly by distracting and pacifying the child. This leisurely maturation process influences the mother's action in feeding . . . Children tend to be dependent, but this is an accepted norm within the culture.

How do we recognize and resolve such dilemmas, when the vast and growing diversity of the families we serve may make the potential for dilemmas seem endless? It is our belief that the best guide for our daily work with children and families is a process approach rather than a recipe, and that such an approach requires us to understand the "deep structure" of culture (Phillips, 1995). But first, let us consider some basic concepts about development and culture.

Development within a Cultural Matrix

We have learned to understand development as a function of the *interrelationships* between the human organism and the environment. The behavioral and developmental capabilities of newborns are modified over time as they make adaptations within the cultural matrix to which they are exposed. At the same time, newborns influence or *shape* their caregivers' responses and, thus, their own caregiving environment. These relationships both promote and limit what we call development.

In this complex process, culture is the mechanism for containing and transmitting the rules for behavior that make it possible for children to participate in a shared meaning system. It is through this participation that children come to have power in the world. Babies, for example, are born with the biological capacity to produce sound; yet not until they come to know the rules that govern speech and language in their culture do they gain the power to communicate. Babies are born with the biological capability to organize information, yet not until they acquire the shared meanings for objects and events do they gain the *power to reason*. As children become more proficient with the rules governing their world, they become more powerful instruments in their own developmental process.

For infants, this process is realized even in the course of normal, daily routines—like feeding. This activity, while serving a nutritional function, also serves to transmit ideas—not just idiosyncratic ones but *patterns of meaning* that are shared by and embodied in the lifestyles of a larger group.

While broad variations in these patterns between cultures are of interest, as critical to our concern here are the enormous subtleties of this process. The quotations at the beginning of this essay suggest that in addition to race and ethnicity, parents' age, education, and social class play a significant role in how children are fed. To understand fully the layers of meaning surrounding any feeding issue, we need to know about family patterns (maternal and paternal) going back at least a generation. We need to be aware of a host of power/control questions, including whether one parent defers to another in matters of feeding, whom parents regard as ultimate authorities on infant feeding, and parents' feelings about delegating control of children's feeding to other adults.

We can only speculate, for example, about why the traditionally raised Chinese American "thirtysomething" professional quotes her pediatrician's advice not to get "uptight" about what her young children eat at a given meal. Does this have something to do with Chinese respect for professional learning? Does it reflect the tendency of professionals to credit their colleague's expertise in his specialty? Would this mother quote the advice of a pediatrician whose recommendations ran counter to her own instincts? And what do the grandparents think?

Michelle, the young African American mother, tells clearly that her own mother's influence far outweighs any recommendation that a pediatrician might make about feeding her new baby. This twenty-year-old still lives at home, and even though Morgan is clearly her child, Michelle appreciates her mother's guidance and support. Michelle had initially planned to breastfeed her daughter, although she reported that most of her friends never even think about breastfeeding. The minor problems she experienced are not unusual, nor is it rare for a newborn to be uninterested in eating. What would have happened if nursing staff or Michelle's mother had given her this information, or encouraged her to persist in breastfeeding?

If Linda Levy's relaxed attitudes about feeding are becoming typical in her subculture, a whole line of "Jewish mother" jokes will be meaningless within a generation.

Residential group care of drug-affected infants may, unfortunately, be emerging as a new subculture in our society. We can observe "cultural rules" being articulated by Mrs. Davis. She says, for example, that it is best to hire staff who have children of their own ("It gives them something to draw on as they work with these children".) She also prefers hiring African American women, since they often "feel like they are giving something back to the community" and this translates into a more stable staffing pattern. Training for staff is not mandated by the state, but is left to each group home owner/operator. In the home run by Mrs. Davis, staff interactions with children are based on their own parenting style. We observed, for example, that a child who could feed himself with his fingers was discouraged from doing so by staff who preferred him to use a spoon, which he could not manage easily. His eating was disrupted by the resulting confrontations. Interaction between two boys being fed at the same time was not encouraged. In fact, if staff had viewed interaction as interfering with the children's eating, they would probably have actively discouraged it.

Feeding is, of course, only one aspect of nurturing. In fact, the notion of infant "feeding" as distinct phenomena may itself be culture-bound. In their study of maternal sensitivity among Laotian Hmong immigrants to the United States, for example, Muret-Wagstaff and Moore observed that Hmong mothers feed their infants continuously (as opposed to on a schedule). They express affection by nuzzling (as opposed to kissing and stroking); they greet babies with vocalization and smiles, waiting for a response and imitating, (as opposed to actively seeking vocal face-to-face interactions—alternately stimulating and soothing precisely in tune with the baby's state of arousal [Muret-Wagstaff & Moore, 1989].) These observations suggest the intricacies with which mothers, by reinforcing certain behaviors and ignoring others, communicate to their children the Hmong way of being in the world, and in turn the subtle ways babies learn to shape their interactions and impact in it. One can only marvel at the complexity of these exchanges and wonder about their meaning.

Subtleties of interaction within relationships make up the developmental process, and the empowering elements in relationships are precisely what we want to ensure for children. As practitioners, we must become better at understanding cultural messages in order to ensure their continuity, provide for their consistency and intervene to prevent any potential disruptions in the process. But how?

Principles for Observing Dimensions of Culture

In the absence of a mature body of literature to guide our practice, we must become better observers ourselves. We must use our day to day work with children to sharpen our understanding about culture. This starts with knowing *what* to look for and *how* to discuss what we see. Having a good technical definition of culture might help, but it is not as necessary to our practice as having a general sense about culture as a force.

Described below are six important concepts that have been helpful in our own struggles to understand the "deep structure" of culture (Phillips, 1995). They are dimensions of culture that are most commonly misunderstood. Awareness of them helps facilitate our ability to observe human behavior and to discuss what we see.

1. *Culture is a set of rules for behavior. (We tend to think of culture as something concrete.)* You cannot "see" culture because you cannot see rules; you can only see the products of culture, in the sense that you can see the behaviors the rules produce. Yet, cultural rules do not cause behavior, they *influence* people to behave similarly, in ways which help them to understand each other.

It is by understanding your culture's rules that you know how to greet a person younger than you, older than you, a friend, a stranger. Cultural rules help you to know *how* to hold a baby. Cultural rules shape food preferences, and celebrations—govern whether you celebrate the sun or the moon; whether you wear a dress or pants, or nothing at all. These rules give meaning to all the events and experiences of life. The essence of culture is not these behaviors themselves, but the rules that produce the behaviors.

2. *Culture is characteristic of groups. (We tend to think of culture mainly in terms of how it affects the individual.)* The rules of a culture are shared by the group, not invented by the individual; the rules of the *group* which are passed on from one generation to the next form the core of the culture. It is a mistake to confuse individual differences with group cultural differences. Every person develops a unique personality as a result of her or his personal history, yet at the same time develops within a cultural context with some behavioral characteristics which are shared with other members of the group. The things we have in common with all humans are the universal, how we differ one from another are the individual, and what we share with members of our group are the cultural.

3. *Culture is learned. (Culture is sometimes confused with race or ethnicity.)* No one is born acculturated; rather, we are born with a biological capability to learn. *What* each person learns depends upon the cultural rules of the people who raise them. Some rules are taught with words "hold your fork in your right hand, and your knife in your left." Other rules are demonstrated by actions—when to smile, how close to stand when talking to someone.

Because culture is learned, it is a mistake to infer a person's culture from his or her appearance. Someone can be *racially* black and *culturally* Irish. A person can also become bi-cultural or tri-cultural by learning the rules of cultures other than his or her own primary group.

4. *Individual members of a culture are embedded to different degrees within their culture (This is the answer to someone who insists, "There's no such thing as Black culture, because all Black people aren't alike.")* Because culture is learned, it can be well learned by some people in the group and less well learned by others. As children are acculturated they usually learn the core rules of their culture, yet they may not always learn every cultural rule equally well. Some families are more tradition-oriented, others less. Further, even though families and individuals learn the cultural rules, they may not always behave according to what they have learned—some people are conformists, others are non-conformists. As a consequence of both phenomena, we say that the behavior of members of a culture will vary depending upon how deeply embedded his or her experiences are within the core of a culture. As we work with individual families, thinking about behavioral variations in this way helps us understand why for instance, all Japanese people don't always "act Japanese."

5. *Cultures borrow and share rules. (This is the answer to the question, "If cultures are different one from another, then why are we alike in some many ways?")* Every cultural group has its own set of core behavioral rules and is therefore unique; yet cultural boundaries overlap and some of the rules of Culture A may be the same as the rules of Culture B. This happens because cultural rules evolve and change over time; sometimes when two groups have extensive contact with one another, they influence each other in some areas. Thus two groups of people may speak the same language, yet have different rules about roles for women. Understanding this helps us avoid discounting the significance of culture just because a person from another culture is so much like you in some ways.

6. *Members of a cultural group may be proficient at following cultural rules but unable to describe them. (Thus the question, "Would you please tell me about your culture?" is unlikely to yield the information you need.)* Acculturation is a natural process. As we become acculturated we are not conscious that our ideas and behavior are being shaped by a unique set of rules. Just as a four-year-old who is proficient with language couldn't, if asked, diagram a sentence or explain the rules of grammar, so also do people become thoroughly proficient with cultural behavior without consciously knowing that they are behaving according to rules. Understanding acculturation in this way explains why you can't walk up to a person and ask him to teach you his culture. Nor could you probably explain your own.

Empowering Young Children through Cultural Consistency

Keeping these principles in mind will help us begin to open the dialogue within settings where children are developing. Insofar as our goal is to provide settings outside their homes that are empowering contexts for children, then the aim of this dialogue ought to be ensuring cultural consistency so their power can be transferred from one setting to the other.

To do so requires several strategies:

1. Observe parents with their own children. Find out what children are familiar with. Practice and imitate what you see. Think about your own cultural style and how it differs from other people's. Have someone watch you and tell you what they see.

2. Discuss culture and how it influences development—staff together, staff with parents, staff with experts. Create an open climate for questions and an open climate for tentative answers. Ask simple questions—what do you expect when other people feed your child? Keep the perspective that people are experts on their own lives. Be aware of power advantage you have over parents. Ask yourself, how can I become more effective in getting information from clients/patients/parents who would never disagree with me face to face? Use informants. Be reflective. De-center: become more insightful about your own culture and how it influences your own development. Don't believe everything you read. Work to identify situations where ethnocentrism is at work.

3. Be prepared for contradictions and conflict. Deal with them as they emerge. (What should you do when you believe some feeding practice contributes to health problems or cultural tradition is not "developmentally appropriate?" Are you perpetuating cultural hegemony by asking someone to change his or her culture?) Don't look for a "recipe solution." Design temporary resolutions. Study the impact of your decisions. Evaluate your progress and change your plans if they aren't working. Create a new knowledge base. Write about it. Share it with the rest of the field.

This dialogue will yield the new ideas that all of us need to understand the cultural dimensions of young children's development. Ongoing dialogue will help all concerned about the well-being of young children and their families to ensure that they will thrive in our country's cultural diversity.

References

Aquino, Conseuelo, J.R.N., M.P.H. 1981. The Filipino in America. *Culture and Childbearing.* Ann L. Clark, R.N., M.A. (ed.). Philadelphia: F.A. Davis Company.

Muret-Wagstaff, Sharon, and Shirley G. Moore "The Hmong in American Infant Behavior and Practices" in Nugent, J. Kevin, Barry Lester and T. Berry Brazelton, editors (1989). *The Cultural Context of Infancy, Volume one: Biology, Culture, and Infant Development.* Ablex Publishing Corporation Norwood, NJ. pp. 319–340.

Nugent, J. Kevin, Barry Lester and T. Berry Brazelton, editors (1989) *The Cultural Context of Infancy, Volume one: Biology, Culture, and Infant Development.* Ablex Publishing Corporation, Norwood, NJ.

Phillips, Carol Brunson (1992) "The promises of diversity: Multicultural challenges and opportunities." *National Louis University Bulletin,* Volume 10, No 1. Evanston, IL. pp. 1–2.

Phillips, Carol Brunson (1995) "Culture: a process that empowers in *Infant/Toddler Caregiving: A Guide to Culturally Sensitive Care,* Peter Mangione editor. California Department of Education, Sacramento, CA. pp. 2–9.

Phillips, Carol Brunson (1988) "Nurturing diversity for today's children and tomorrow's leaders." *Young Children,* Volume 43, No 2. Washington, DC. pp. 42–47.

Questions about Reading 18

1. Were you aware of any feelings arising as you read this article?

2. When dilemmas arise over differing ideas about feeding practices, the authors state that their approach is a process approach rather then a recipe. What do you think they mean?

S leeping is another area where families and caregivers may not see eye to eye. Janet Gonzalez-Mena and Navaz Peshotan Bhavnagri explore that issue in their article "Cultural Differences in Sleeping Practices".

Reading 19

....

Cultural Differences in Sleeping Practices

by Janet Gonzalez-Mena and Navaz Peshotan Bhavnagri

Janet Gonzalez-Mena has been a pre-school teacher, child care director, and a teacher educator. She also writes books and articles about early childhood education. One of her books is Dragon Mom, *which grew out of the Exchange article "Mrs. Godzilla Takes on the Child Development Experts."*

Navaz Peshotan Bhavnagri, Ph.D., is an associate professor of early childhood education at Wayne State University, Detroit, Michigan. She has served the field of early childhood education for 38 years. She has diverse work experiences in Houston, New York, Detroit, West Lafayette, Champaign-Urbana, and India.

A fifteen-month-old from a Southeast Asian refugee family lay screaming in a crib in a child care center. This baby who had never slept alone in his life entered child care where, like all babies in that program, he was put down for a nap in a crib. This child experienced cultural shock. His screams were so intense that he was finally picked up. He wouldn't stop screaming until he was taken out of the nap room and put back in the playroom. Of course, nap time can be upsetting for any baby or child for that matter, whether it's a cross-cultural experience or not. Being expected to sleep in a strange place can be disturbing no matter what the child's age or background. However, if the child is not from the mainstream culture, then that information needs to be factored into the staff's understanding of nap time upsets.

Out-of-home, cross-cultural child care is expanding more rapidly than ever. That means even more children are now facing huge changes in their lives as programs implement regulations and policies which are in direct contrast to what the parents do at home. The question of how to be developmentally appropriate and yet at the same time remain culturally sensitive is an important one, especially when the parents' practices and program policies are at odds with each other. What kind of parent education can professionals provide when parents have different ideas from those who run the program? If a parent has a question about sleeping, how can you answer it without understanding her traditions and beliefs?

Given that so many parents have questions about putting children to bed and keeping them there, it is easy to assume those are universal questions. The issue is separation—and separation during sleep is not practiced by everybody. In some cultures where co-sleeping is the norm, bedtime and night wakings are not considered problems. Children don't come into their parents' bed in the night because they are already there, or if not in bed with a parent, in bed with someone else (sibling or grandparent). Children who co-sleep don't necessarily sleep through the night and they aren't expected to. But they don't wake up alone, so there is no separation issue and therefore usually much less sleep disturbance to either child or the sleeping companion.

Co-sleeping itself can become an issue when parents put their children into child care, and the children have never slept by themselves before like the little boy in the opening vignette. Of course, not all children freak out the way he did, but staff may still notice some effects. For example, when children are used to much more physical contact than they get in child care they may miss it when it's lacking. Babies, for instance, are never without human contact in some cultures because they are held day and night at home. Child care is bound to be a different experience for those babies.

That doesn't mean that staff have to hold children all day every day. A solution may be just a matter of holding infants until they go to sleep or rubbing the back of a preschooler. Or it may be teaching them a different way of going to sleep.

In any case, understanding how child care is different from home is important. Staff needs to know that in families where babies never sleep alone their parents may be shocked to find their babies off in a dark room, confined in a crib, with no human contact. They may think it unduly harsh to expect preschool children to lie by themselves on a cot a few feet from other children and not be allowed to touch them.

Although early childhood professionals may consider that sleeping alone is the norm and should be the goal for all children, that's a very strange goal in minds of some parents. Some consider the practice the very opposite of good care! The challenge to the caregivers and those who set program policy is to recognize that co-sleeping is an accepted practice in most parts of the world. Thus, it is not the norm world-wide. Indeed, what is considered *normal*, *effective*, and *optimal* is based on an extremely small sample of the world's population. The standard setters in the western world are influenced by the perspectives of middle-class people of European extraction.

Of course, when it comes to co-sleeping, it doesn't take much research to discover it is also common practice among many families in the United States who think it's bad but do it anyway. They know the parenting books frown on the practice, so some parents do it and feel guilty and others do it and keep quiet about it. It is important for staff to know that in spite of parenting books, co-sleeping is not only considered normal by large numbers of people, but healthy and desirable as well.

Before professionals give advice to families about sleeping arrangements, they should recognize that sleeping arrangements are strongly mandated by value-laden cultural customs. Where advice about cultural customs comes from varies with the family. Some parents go to books for their advice. Others go to elders. Still others don't have to go anywhere because child rearing has been such a part of their lives from childhood on that they know what to do without seeking advice.

Some parents seek advice from many sources. The problem is that sometimes professionals give advice on issues such as sleeping without understanding the cultural context. For example, one visiting European-American early childhood expert was asked by a Navajo mother about when and how to take her baby out of his cradleboard. He only used it for sleeping at this point in his life, but she was concerned that he had stayed in it too long because he had literally outgrown it. His feet hung over the edge and the thongs strapping him in had to be lengthened. But whenever nap time came in the center, he immediately toddled over to his cradleboard and asked to get into it. The center had no policy on cradleboards. It would have been presumptuous for this early childhood professional to do any more than listen to the mother and help her sort out her concerns. If advice were called for, it needed to come from a Navajo elder, not an Anglo visiting from another part of the country.

There are times that advice is called for. Sometimes there are mandates related to health and sanitation issues, for example. Then, of course, there are regulations and standards. But before giving advice or explaining mandated regulations to families, professionals need to understand the family and the cultural context, and they need to be up on cross-cultural research.

There is some interesting research, for example, that points to the benefits of co-sleeping. Meredith Small, an anthropologist, makes a case for co-sleeping in her book, *Our Babies Ourselves*. She writes about how human contact during sleep assists infants in regulating their body temperature, breathing, and heart rate during the first weeks, even months, of life. Mothers' and infants' sleep cycles and states are synchronized with each other when they sleep together. They lose this synchrony when they sleep apart. Crib death or Sudden Infant Death Syndrome (SIDS) rates are very low or almost nonexistent in cultures where co-sleeping is commonly practiced. Another benefit of co-sleeping is that it makes breast feeding more convenient. Further, children who sleep with someone are less likely to need "transitional objects" such as a special blanket or stuffed animal.

Of course, there are also cultural values beliefs, priorities, and goals to consider. In families where close contact is more important than early independence, co-sleeping fits. In those families that have priority of independence and individuality starting at a young age, co-sleeping may be seen as a step away from their goals.

We're not advocating co-sleeping in centers. We're not urging anyone to violate policies or health standards. We are asking only that programs and staff to try to understand a family whose sleeping practices don't fit with those of the center, instead of just imposing on them the standard accepted practice. When family and program experience a cultural bump around sleeping practices professionals need to ask themselves whether they really understand the cultural issues involved. Has there been a conversation about the family's goals for the child? If yes, does the practice fit the goals? Is there a risk factor in the family's practice? Surely if there is sound research that indicates a risk factor, it's the professional's responsibility to tell the family.

To understand cultural differences staff and families must communicate with each other. Communication is a prerequisite for looking for a creative solution that incorporates both the parents' and caregivers' concerns. This approach fits right in with the "both/and thinking" explained in NAEYC's revised book, *Developmentally Appropriate Practice in Early Childhood Programs*. According to authors Sue Bredekamp and Carol Copple, professionals can and should avoid the polarization of "either/or choices" and explore thoroughly how two seemingly opposing views can both be right.

It may be hard to explore a situation where there is a clear conflict of values between what's behind the program policy, professional standards or state regulations, and what's behind the parents' practices. But with openness to diversity and a dedication to respecting all perspectives, relationships between professionals and families grow. With a good and trusting relationship, professionals and families can use creative ways to find common ground. It's in the child's best interests that the two groups responsible for her care work together in harmony and understanding.

References

For further information: American Academy of Pediatrics. www.aap.org; National Institute of Child Health and Human Development. *www.nichd.nih.gov.*

Bhavnagri, N. P, and Gonzalez-Mena, J. (1997). The cultural context of infant caregiving. *Childhood Education, 74,* 1, 2–8.

Bredekamp, S., and Copple, C. (1997). *Developmentally Appropriate Practice in Early Childhood Programs.* Washington, DC: NAEYC.

Gantley, M., Davies, D. R, & Murcett, A. (1993). Sudden infant death syndrome: Links with infant care practices. *British Medical Journal, 306,* 16–20.

Kawaski, C., Nugent, J. K., Miyashita, H., Miyahara, H., & Brazelton, T. B. (1994). The cultural organization of infants' sleep. *Children's Environments, 11,* 135–141.

Latz, S., Wolf, A W., Lozoff, B. (1999). Co-sleeping in context: Sleep practices and problems in young children in Japan and the United States. *Pediatrics & Adolescent Medicine, 153,* 339–346.

Lozoff, B., Askew, G. L., Wolf, A. W. (1996). Co-sleeping and early childhood sleep problems: Effects of ethnicity and socioeconomic status. *Developmental and Behavioral Pediatrics, 17(1),* 9–15.

McKenna, J. J., & Mosko, S. (1993). Evolution and infant sleep: An experimental study of infant-parent co-sleeping and its implications for SIDS. *Acta Paediatrica Supplement, 389*, 31–36.

Morelli, G. A., Rogoff, B., Oppenheim, D., & Goldsmith, D. (1992). Culture variation in infants' sleeping arrangements: Questions of independence. *Developmental Psychology, 28*, 604–613.

Small, M. (1998). *Our Babies Ourselves: How biology and culture shape the way we parent.* New York: Anchor Books.

Wolf, A. W., Lozoff, B., Latz, S., & Paludetto, R (1996). Parental theories in the management of sleep routines in Japan, Italy, and the United States. In S. Harkness & C. M. Super (Eds.), *Parents cultural belief systems* (pp. 364–385). New York: Guilford.

Questions about Reading 19

1. What are your experiences with different ideas about how to put infants and toddlers to sleep and keep them asleep?

2. Co-sleeping is perhaps more widely practiced than many families let on. What do you think about infants and toddlers sleeping with someone rather than in their own crib or bed?

3. How might sleeping practices be related to cultural values?

4. What do you think is the point of this article? Do you think the authors are trying to get child care programs to change their policies around sleeping practices?

Readings on Including Infants and Toddlers with Special Needs

The first article, "Talking with Parents When Concerns Arise," by Linda Brault and Janet Gonzalez-Mena, discusses what caregivers can do to get help and support when they find that they having difficulties meeting the needs of a particular child.

Reading 20

···

Talking with Parents when Concerns Arise

Linda Brault, MA, Sonoma State University and Janet Gonzalez-Mena, MA

Marta cared for six children in her home. Rashad, nearly eight months old, was enrolled by his parents, Suzanne and Paul, when he was six months old. Rashad was their first child. Marta was beginning to be concerned about Rashad's development. Rashad was a very happy, contented baby. However, he seemed almost too content to Marta. He could sit up when placed, but hadn't shown much interest in moving by himself. When Marta asked Suzanne or Paul how things were going, they seemed very thankful for such a "good" baby. Marta wondered if she should say anything about her worries. Maybe Rashad was just a "good" baby.

Sarali attended ABC child care center. She was nearly three years old and had been at the center for one year. Emily, her teacher, had just taken a class at the local community college about child development. During the class, she found herself thinking about Sarali. She was always in need of her attention. She often was in the middle of things when other children were hurt or upset. Emily wondered what it was about Sarali that made her stand out from the other children. Her father, José, had two older children and he was always rushed during drop-off or pick-up. José certainly didn't seem worried. Why was Emily?

As a child care provider, you are often the first one to notice a child who learns or communicates differently than other children in your care. If your careful observation and efforts to work effectively with a particular child do not seem to be meeting the child's needs, it is time to look for help to foster belonging and appropriately support this child in your program. This help can come from the family, but more expertise may be needed, such as from the child's pediatrician or health care provider, a therapist or another specialist.

When you recommend to the family that they seek help in this way, or if you get their permission to seek that help yourself, you are "making a referral." It is easiest if the family makes the referral, as they will have the information needed and can get the process started most quickly. In order for you to make a referral to health, education or early intervention systems, you will need to talk to the parents of the child first. They must give their written permission (consent) before you seek other assistance.

Sometimes parents will notice the developmental differences on their own. Although comparing one child with another can be a disservice to both, it often helps parents to have a broader view than they may have if their experience is limited to their own child.

Portions of this material were used in: Brault, L.M.J. (In Press) *Making Inclusion Work: Strategies to Promote Belonging for Children with Special Needs in Child Care Settings.* Sacramento: California Department of Education, Child Development Division.

One mother of a baby who was born with a serious heart defect entered an infant/toddler program that had a parent observation component. She was shocked when she saw the difference in development between her son and the other children his age. Because of his fragile condition and several surgeries, his early experiences had been very different from other children his age in this program. This mother didn't need the caregiver to recommend a referral. She went immediately to the heart specialist, and the pediatrician to ask for help with her son's developmental needs. She understood that when specialists are worried about saving a baby's life, their concerns about over-all development go on hold sometimes. With the help of the caregiver and a developmental specialist, the child moved from being seen primarily as a heart patient to being a developing toddler.

That case was unusual because the parent didn't need a referral. She already had specialists to help her and ultimately the program as well. What about children like Rashad and Sarali? If the concern you have is for a child who isn't already defined as a child with special needs, you may not know how the parents will react when you share your concerns.

Sharing Concerns

How do you decide when to have a formal conference to talk to parents about your concerns? If you have spent some time focusing on the child and clarifying your concerns, you can ask the parents to schedule an uninterrupted time for you to talk with them. If you have worked to establish a good relationship with the parents, you probably have been talking to them all along, so you know if the issues you are worried about are unique to your setting or if the parents have noticed the same at home. You may know that the parents are concerned as well, and that their concerns are the same as yours. You may also know if they have not expressed any worries and can take that into account in planning.

Certainly if there have been regular small conversations, the conference itself won't come as a surprise to the parents. Nevertheless, if you decide that the time has come to get some outside help by making a referral, this conference may take on deeper significance than the usual parent-caregiver conference or the casual conversations you've been having with the parents.

Preparing for a Conference

Prepare for a more formal conference by making careful observations of the child. Observation of the child over time will give you information about specific behaviors that illustrate the concern. It will help you clarify a general concern (*Rashad seems too easygoing; Sarali is always in the middle of trouble*) with specific examples of behavior (*Rashad stays in one position for up to thirty minutes and doesn't change positions on his own; Sarali has trouble sitting at the table during snack time and often hits children*). Note when and where those behaviors occur and under what circumstances. With focused observation you may get some insights into what is contributing to the behavior. See if changing the environment or your approach affects the behavior. Keep track of all the details of what you have tried and what happened. This record can contain important information to share with the parents.

Remember it is only appropriate for you to discuss what you have observed about *specific behaviors*. Avoid the urge to label or diagnose. Sometimes parents have noticed that their child's development is different from most children and they come to the conference feeling relief that someone has noticed. They may come anticipating that they will get the help and support they need. Other times parents may be unaware of differences or unable to see them. If parents haven't noticed anything, it may be a different situation.

Conducting the Conference

In the meeting itself, do what you can to make the parents feel comfortable and at ease as much as possible. Choose a seating arrangement that brings you together instead of separating you. Sitting behind a desk,

Beginning Observations of Rashad

Marta thought about Rashad and what other infants his age were like. Marta decided to focus on his movement. She would make a note with the time and what position Rashad was placed in for three days. Marta noticed that Rashad would stay in whatever position he was put in (on his back, on his stomach or sitting up) for at least thirty minutes, sometimes longer without fussing. Rashad only rolled over from his stomach to his back only one time in the three days Marta was keeping track. He did fall over from sitting sometimes when an older child rushed by and Rashad tried to turn his head too fast. Rashad spent time watching the other children and looking at toys, but rarely picked toys or objects up. Marta noted that she had been changing Rashad's position without realizing it several times a day.

Beginning Observations of Sarali

When Emily asked her aide about Sarali, she said she "behaved badly and bothered other children" but Emily knew that description alone would not be helpful to her parents. She decided to watch her carefully for an entire week so that she could give specifics. Emily noticed that Sarali had a harder time sitting still than other children did. She counted the times Sarali got up during snack and was able to give the actual figures of 2 times on Monday, Tuesday and Wednesday, 5 times on Thursday and 1 time on Friday. Her interactions with children could also be observed and described. When Sarali was playing with more than one other child Emily observed and recorded five incidents of hitting other children during the past week. She also noticed that Sarali had fewer words and phrases than other almost-three year olds.

for example, can make a psychological as well as a physical barrier between you and the parents. A warmer, friendlier arrangement may work better. Provide for privacy. This meeting is between you and the parents, not the business of the secretary or the rest of the staff. If you are a family child care provider you may need to meet outside of regular hours of care. Set aside enough time so that the meeting isn't rushed and you can talk things through. If this is the first such meeting the parents have had, they need to feel that you care and that they can trust you.

Start by asking the family how they see their child's development and share any positive qualities you have observed. Ask about how the child behaves at home. If the family differs in their view of the child, be open to their perspective, ask questions, gather information and invite them to be your partners in meeting the needs of their child. When done respectfully, this communication can lead to a better exchange of ideas and ultimately be of most help to the child.

Before you share your concerns with them, ask if they have any that they haven't already indicated. When it is time to share your concerns, let the family know that you are sharing your concerns to support their child's development and to get some ideas for how to best meet their child's needs. Be sure you communicate what you want to say clearly, without judgment and with concrete examples. It is especially important that you share your observations without labeling or diagnosing. DO NOT suggest that a child has a specific diagnosis (such as attention deficit disorder). Most child care providers are not qualified to provide such a diagnosis and doing so often gets in the way of the next steps in the referral process. On the other hand, your specific observations and descriptions of what is happening will be very helpful to any specialists who become involved.

Supporting the Family Who Wants to Access Resources

If the family is also concerned or agrees with your observations, you can move to a discussion of possible next steps. Support the family in getting help. Their biggest fear is often that you will reject their child or them if extra help is needed. Let them know that you are there to support their child and to incorporate any new ideas. You should have information ready about services within your program, local early intervention services, special education services and other resources. By sharing your concrete observations, you will be able to help the family clarify their questions about their child and what the referral will accomplish.

When ready to refer to the early intervention program, local school district, or pediatrician/healthcare provider, let the family take the lead. Since many families will want to take action, be prepared to talk with them about resources for obtaining further assessment and/or possible services. This is the point at which you are "making a referral." It is generally appropriate to refer the family to their pediatrician at the same time you refer them to the local early intervention and/or special education resources.

Calling resource agencies ahead of time to gather general information can be very helpful. However, you cannot guarantee eligibility or services from another agency to a family. Rather, describe what might happen after the referral and what the possible outcomes might be based on what you've learned. You can also let the family know that you can be a source of information to the referral source. Parents must give permission for you to talk about their child with health and educational referral sources, so you will want to carefully respect the family's confidentiality and be sure that you have clear consent.

When the family wants to access other resources, being aware of potential barriers can smooth their path. Some barriers include issues of insurance, spoken language of the family, cultural practices, transportation and discomfort or previous negative experiences with authority figures such as teachers or doctors. It is not uncommon for a child care provider to help the families obtain services their child needs by setting the process in motion for them. Be careful not to do too much for the family, however. Rather than feeling responsible for overcoming the barrier, you can focus on supporting the family as they encounter a barrier. For example, a family can make the call to the referral source from your office, with you there to provide support and clarification if needed. Finding ways for the family to meet their child's needs will serve the family and their child best in the long run.

When the Family Chooses Not to Access Resources

If the parents don't understand what your concerns are, think they are not important, or disagree with your observation, they may be upset if you suggest that a referral is necessary. It's even possible that your observations will shock or anger them. In this case, sensitively supporting the parents' feelings is called for without getting caught up in them. When infants and toddlers are distressed, caregivers accept the feelings and empathize with the child. Parents need the same approach from caregivers.

You are not a therapist, but some of the listening skills of a therapist can serve you well. For example, if the parents get angry, your immediate response may be to get defensive and argue your case. If you get caught up in your own feelings, you are less available to give parents the support they need at a time when they are vulnerable. Understanding that anger or blame are common responses for people in pain helps you accept the feelings without taking them personally. You may feel an urge to come back with your own feelings, but this is the time to focus on those of the parents and listen to what they have to say without minimizing their upset feelings or trying to talk them out of it. Keep clear that further assessment is a positive move and that both you and the parents have the child's best interests at heart even if you don't see eye-to-eye at the moment.

Sometimes the family may not choose to access resources when you first share your concerns, or they may be open to information yet not take action immediately. Rather than label them as being "in denial" or something else, remember that everyone moves at a different pace and accepts information differently. The family's emotional response will affect what they are able to hear and understand. Processing and integrating this information will take varying amounts of time. The reality that life will have to change—that their child may be different than other children—is very hard for some families to hear.

Unless behavior or other issues, such as medical urgency, will prevent you from caring for the child without assistance, allow the family to proceed on their own time line. Be prepared to support them in understanding what you have shared, repeating the information whenever necessary. Let them know that there is resource information available whenever they want it. If you find that your own judgment or emotions about this interfere with your ability to respect the family as the decision-maker, seek support for yourself and don't be afraid to suggest that the family discuss this with someone else as well.

If you believe that not seeking help is an issue of neglect and the child will be harmed, then you do have an obligation to be clear with the family and make an appropriate referral yourself to a child protective agency. Referrals to child protective agencies do not require parent consent.

Resources for Families

Health and medical service systems

In many cases it is appropriate to have a family talk about their concerns with their primary health care provider. Certain issues faced by children with disabilities or other special needs are medical in nature and will require careful follow-up by a health care provider. Some health care providers specialize in working with children with special needs, while others have limited knowledge of the assessment and service issues.

Parents and providers must be proactive to assure a good match between the child and the primary health care provider. It is often a good idea for the referral to be made to the special education and/or early intervention service system at the same time as the referral to the health care provider, since the referral process takes time and referring only to one system (such as health care) may delay the entry to the other (such as early intervention). Remember, referrals are best made directly by the family. If a provider makes a referral, the family must have provided clear permission.

Local special education and/or early intervention service systems

Local special education and/or early intervention service systems are required by law to engage in "Child Find." In other words, there is supposed to be an active and ongoing effort on the part of the specialist system to identify children who may be eligible for services. Some areas may provide free screenings at local child care settings, while others may send outreach materials to child care and medical agencies. Not all children with differences in their development will qualify for services from special education and/or early intervention. This is determined after appropriate screening and assessment. This assessment is provided to families free of charge, as are most special education services. After referral, the special education and/or early intervention agency has 45 calendar days (50 for children over three) to complete the assessment, determine eligibility and hold a meeting to plan for service if needed. Again, referrals are best made directly by the family.

Once a referral is received, representatives of those agencies will talk with the family and may schedule an assessment to see if the child qualifies for services. Knowing the best contact name and number in your local area can be of great help to the family. Each state is required to have a *Central Directory of Services* for early intervention services. These can be found through the state agency overseeing early intervention in each state. For the name of this agency in your state, visit the National Early Childhood Technical Assistance Center (NECTAC) online at www.nectac.org.

There are legal timelines for responding to parent requests for consideration of early intervention or special education services. Requests by phone usually start the timeline. Parents may also put their request in writing if they are having difficulty getting a response. Parents must give written permission for the child to be tested and receive early intervention or special education. All services are confidential and many are provided at no cost to the family. Even if a child is not found eligible for early intervention or special education services, the team providing the assessment may have suggestions for ways to support the child's growth and development. Additionally, they will be able to give guidelines for monitoring the child's progress as the child becomes older, in case the family or others become concerned.

If the child referred is found eligible and begins to receive early intervention or special education services, the child can benefit from your working with the specialists on his or her team. They can become consultants to you and the family. The open and ongoing communication you have established with the family will serve you well as you continue to exchange information and support the child to become all that he or she can be.

Keeping the Communication Going

As you can see, sharing concerns with a family requires thoughtful, sensitive communication. After the conference, keep the communication going so that you are able to support the family to support their child. Connect with any specialists who may work with the child. You are an important partner in the child's development and the information you receive can improve your services for all children.

Next Steps for Rashad

During the conference, Suzanne and Paul shared that while Rashad was a good baby, he didn't seem to be doing things that cousins or babies of friends were doing. When Marta shared her observations with Suzanne and Paul, they were very interested in getting help. They took Rashad to the local community clinic for his well-baby checkups so Marta suggested that they ask the nurse about Rashad's development. Marta also told them about the early intervention program available at no cost. They agreed to call the agency the next day when they dropped Rashad off at Marta's. That way, if they had questions, Marta could help them. Rashad was found eligible for service from the early intervention program and received visits to his home as well as at Marta's home. He began making progress and Marta learned several new ways to help Rashad's development.

Next Steps for Sarali

Sarali's father, José, was surprised to hear that Sarali was having difficulty in school. He reported that she seemed to do fine at home and wondered if she was just used to older brothers who "dished it out as well as took it." José reminded Emily that his wife, Rosa, was in the military and had been gone more than she was home for the past year, which made things more hectic for all of them. José felt that this was just a temporary problem and not something to be worried about. Emily asked José if he had any ideas about helping Sarali sit during snack. José said that Sarali was an active girl and wondered if Emily could let her clear the table or do something else to let her move around. Emily said that she would think about what seemed to help and did remember that the day Sarali only got up once was when the children were putting the snack together, so perhaps a more active snack role would help her. Emily remained concerned that Sarali's language seemed behind and wondered if that contributed to her hitting instead of using words with other children. José agreed to talk to the pediatrician. The pediatrician thought that Sarali would probably start using more words soon, and did not think that more treatment was needed at this time. Emily continued to carefully observe Sarali and made some changes in her snack time. Sarali was able to sit for longer times at snack when she had more to do. Emily assigned her aide to be near Sarali during large group activities and they were able to decrease some of the hitting. Sarali's language did not seem to be progressing, but Emily knew she could share her specific concerns at the next conference.

Questions about Reading 20

1. What does it mean to make a referral?

2. How do you decide when it is time to set up a conference with the family to discuss your concerns about their child?

3. What are some ways to create a warm, friendly, and private environment for the conference?

4. Why should you describe specific behaviors that concern you when you talk to the family?

5. From what you know about Rashad, would you be concerned about him too? What do you think about how Rashad is put into a sitting position? Knowing that Magda Gerber warns caregivers and parents to avoid putting infants in positions they can't get into by themselves, would you make an exception to Gerber's rule in Rashad's case?

Children with special needs are children first. Caregivers should always keep that fact in mind and not let the disability define the child. As you read, pay attention to how the careful wording in this article always puts the child first and the disability second in the sentence. Notice how this article starts by focusing on *all* children, *and* includes those with disabilities. Notice too that an underlying theme is individualization. The many different strategies in this article will give you ideas about how to help and support infants and toddlers who have special needs when they are in child care and education settings with their typically developing peers.

Reading 21

Strategies for Supporting Infants and Toddlers with Disabilities in Inclusive Child Care

by Donna Sullivan & Janet Gonzalez-Mena

Introduction

Many strategies work for all infants and toddlers including those with special needs and disabilities. This first section is a general outline of strategies for setting up environments, managing the essential activities of daily living (such as caregiving routines), and encouraging free play and exploration. The second section deals with strategies for specific disabilities. That section does not stand alone, however, because it is only complete when coupled with the first section. Also, it is important to remember that children don't fit into "neat " categories and children with disabilities are not defined by their disability. Multiple strategies will often be most effective.

General Strategies

Communication

The communication needs of very young children with disabilities are similar to their typically developing peers. Sensitive caregivers are "watchers" and listeners, while also giving children appropriate information and responses without being overly talkative or intrusive. Children need responsive adults who respond with warmth and who are linguistically appropriate. They need adults who communicate feelings and information. Primarily they need adults and caregivers who are **there** for them.

LEARNING FROM FAMILIES

Talking with families helps us to better understand young children especially if there is a communication need. It is particularly important to find out how the child communicates at home. How does she tell you she is wet, hungry, sad, worried, etc.? Families are a rich source in regard to the ways their child shares information.

SOUL TECHNIQUE

When we think about how adults enter into conversations (and interactions) with young children, one of the strategies that can be used is *SOUL*. *SOUL* has four components: *Silence*, *Observation*, *Understanding*, and *Listening*. These are techniques that encourage partnerships in conversations with young children by supporting a child's initiation, allowing a child time to respond, practicing good observation of children's skills and intentions, and becoming an effective listener (with your ears, your eyes, and your heart).

Silence allows us time to watch and listen to better understand the child's perspective. This comes before talking and reminds the adult to follow the child's lead and provide authentic responses. The "lead" may be very subtle—a glance, a slight movement of a hand, an averted gaze.

Observation helps us learn where a child's interests are. *Observation* also gives us cues for adaptations or modifications within the environment and ways that we can extend a child's play.

Understanding encourages adults to look at things from the child's perspective: his approach, how he problem solves, his comprehension. Think about puzzles: what happens when you tell him to *turn* a puzzle piece? Does he turn it over? Around? As children try things in different ways, using their own strategies, they are communicating with those around them. It is important for us to validate and check for understanding, even with the youngest child. Children feel competent when we understand their messages, verbal or otherwise. Communicative competence leads to self confidence.

Listening can be supported in a number of ways: proximity, ears, eye contact, body language, and our affect and demeanor. Really *Listening* allows us to follow the child's lead, pace, etc. It means that we don't interrupt as soon as we think we understand. In the case of some children, it means that we allow a little extra "wait" time for processing.

Pacing

During caregiving routines, those essential "activities of daily living," keep the pace unhurried and allow infants and toddlers as much time as they need to be as independent as they can. Encourage them to use their developing skills at whatever level possible. Individualize so that no child feels hurried. Talk to the child about what is going to happen and look for any indication of understanding. Allow plenty of time for the child to do whatever may be needed to contribute to the joint effort. In the face of difficulty, support the child in his efforts to keep trying, even when frustration arises, but be sensitive about what frustration level is too much.

During play allow infants and toddlers as much time as they need to accomplish whatever they are trying to do. Encourage them to use the skills they have without rushing them. Pace should be unhurried for all infants and toddlers. Individualize the pace for all children and be reminded that some children may need significantly more time than others.

Providing for play and exploration

All infants and toddlers need to spend a good part of their waking hours in an environment that invites exploration. Safety is a vital consideration when setting up an environment. Safety issues for specific disabilities are included in the next section, along with some ideas and adaptations for helping children whose abilities may be limited for exploration and for those who may need extra encouragement to explore.

Support, encourage, and facilitate interactions with toys. Rather than using direct instruction to show how something works, tickle the child's curiosity and wait to see if he or she will be motivated to explore.

Make a choice of toys and materials accessible in ways that encourage infants and toddlers to use the physical skills they have. Positioning is important if the child is to be comfortable and secure in ways that leave hands free. Encourage children to reach for toys, rather than putting them in their hands.

Support, encourage, and facilitate interactions with peers. Accept different levels of interaction as appropriate to each individual. Sometimes just being near other children is interactive enough.

Multi-sensory experiences

All infants and toddlers need a variety of sensory experiences, but must be protected from overstimulation. It is important for caregivers to recognize individual thresholds. What is not enough stimulation for one child may be too much for another. Also children are drawn to use some senses more than others. It is the thoughtful and sensitive caregiver who finds ways to encourage the use of all senses without forcing or being manipulative with children.

Provide for independence as well as interdependence

In programs where "I did it all by myself" is an important goal, it is also vital to teach the values of accepting help and helping others. All children need to learn that independence and interdependence aren't opposites but two sides of the same coin. Dependence isn't bad! Help children feel good about accepting help and also about giving it. Help children to see how they can sometimes be independent by encouraging self-help skills. Make toys and materials accessible. Further, provide environmental modifications (stairs, ramps, railings) to help toddlers reach changing tables or to get to another level.

Provide for rest when needed

Be extremely sensitive to when individual infants and toddlers need rest and provide for it. Some children don't give clear signals when they've had enough. Find out from parents how they know when their child needs a rest. Be aware of the very different tolerance levels children have for activity. Doing something that seems ordinary for a typically developing child may be fatiguing for children with physical differences or health issues. Just being around other people may fatigue an infant or toddler. Don't postpone a rest period for a child who needs it for the sake of a schedule or a group activity.

Strategies for Supporting Specific Disabilities

The "categories" listed below are provided to facilitate referencing. They are not intended to define children! The strategies came from the authors' life experiences as well as the written sources referenced at the end of this section.

Physical disabilities (orthopedic impairments)

PACE
Encourage the child to become as involved as possible during caregiving routines and exploration periods. "Hurrying" a child with cerebral palsy may increase muscle tone and make an activity like diapering or eat-

ing more difficult. Sudden movements may also be counterproductive. Be reminded that for some children there is a delay between the "intention" to do something and actually doing it.

POSITIONING

Special chairs or positioning equipment may be needed throughout the day, requiring extra space.

Position children who need it so they feel comfortable and secure during routines and play. Find out from parents the best positioning strategies. Think about how a child can be supported but able to exert efforts on his own. Be sensitive to when the position needs to change. Not being able to get out of a position can be frustrating. Be aware that sometimes what seems like a psychological insecurity may, in fact, be a physical insecurity, which may be remedied by correct positioning or support.

PROVIDING FOR MOVEMENT

Familiarize the child with the environment and how best to move within it. Space may be needed to accommodate movement of special equipment such as a walker or a wheelchair. Address safety considerations for a clear path, smooth but not slippery surfaces, and ways around thick rugs inside or sand areas outside. Keep the environment free of clutter.

Though most typically developing children go from crawling to cruising to walking, some children in an inclusive program may need ways to cruise later or longer than typically developing children. Arrange the room so there are supports for cruising such as furniture, tables, rails, or walls to pull up on and use for support when cruising. Make sure these are sturdy and the appropriate height.

PROVIDING FOR PLAY AND EXPLORATION

Place toys within reach, but not necessarily in the infant's or toddler's hand. Encourage the child to reach out or move to low accessible shelves. Be aware of what it does to a child who still has a strong grasp reflex to have a toy put in her hand. She doesn't have a choice to let go, and the toy may become irritating or upsetting to her. "Prying" a child's hand open who has a strong grasp reflex may increase the reflex. Flexing the wrist or other relaxation techniques may be utilized to help the child open her fingers.

Provide toys that children with fine motor involvement can grasp, move, or create an effect by using. Modify toys and materials when necessary (see below).

Support, encourage, and facilitate interactions with toys. Rather than using direct instruction to show how something works, tickle the child's curiosity and wait to see if he or she becomes engaged. Some children with physical disabilities have not had some of the play opportunities that their typically developing peers have had.

Support, encourage, and facilitate interactions with peers. Accept different levels of interaction as appropriate to each individual. Watch for subtle responses. Sometimes just being near other children is interactive enough.

PROTECTION FROM NOISE.

Thought must be given about setting up the environment so that infants and toddlers (who are not mobile) may be in areas where they won't be bothered by loud or sudden noises, such as a telephone, because of the physical effect these can have on the individual.

ADAPTING MATERIALS, TOYS, AND UTENSILS:

- Nonskid materials keep toys and utensils from slipping. Use velcro, dycem pads, and suction soap holders.
- Make handles bigger with foam bike handle grips, cotton pads, "vet wrap," and tape.
- Add handles. For example, place cork stoppers or wooden knobs on puzzle pieces. Example: glue tongue depressors to cardboard book pages for easy turning.
- Bend spoon handles, use flexible straws, and use nontipping or spouted cups with lids to make eating more independent.
- Make holes in beads bigger or use stiffer string (cover end with masking tape).
- Cover paper materials (books, cards) with clear contact paper to make them stiffer and drool proof.
- Use velcro or magnetic blocks.

Visual Impairments

PROVIDING FOR MOVEMENT

Familiarize the child with the environment. Keep room arrangement consistent so infants and toddlers with visual limitations can move more easily. Minimize clutter.

To help crawlers and toddlers navigate the room, look for ways in which they can be as independent as possible by using auditory and tactile cues as guides.

PROVIDING FOR PLAY AND EXPLORATION

Play with "real" objects is especially important for the child with a visual impairment. Concrete learning is critical and the transition between what is real and what is a toy is very difficult without visual input.

Place objects within reach, and help the child know they are there by touch or other types of "cues." Encourage the child to reach out or move to low accessible shelves. Support, encourage, and facilitate interactions with objects. Engage the child's curiosity by selecting items with high contrast or that provide auditory input. Expand play behaviors if play is limited to mouthing or smelling.

Add textured cues (sandpaper, fake fur, vinyl) to help children locate items. Provide toys that children can grasp, move, or create an effect by using. Modify toys and materials when necessary to add auditory elements (a bell in a nerf ball) or additional texture. Adding smells may make toys and objects more identifiable and interesting.

Capitalize on residual visual abilities by using toys that light up (use caution if the child is prone to seizures) or have highly contrasting colors or heavy black outlines. Place objects on something with a high contrast background or defined edge like a tray.

Support, encourage, and facilitate interactions with peers. The child with a visual impairment may not be aware of another child nearby. Adults can support with verbal information and touch. "Direction" words coupled with touch (such as left and right) can be used early on to help toddlers determine location.

PROTECTION FROM NOISE AND CONFUSION

Provide space that has reduced noise and movement for children who may have difficulty discriminating and staying focused.

Hearing Impairments

MULTI-SENSORY EXPERIENCES

- Use multi-sensory cues.
- Use visual and tactile cues to help guide the infant or toddler in daily routines and activities.
- Use picture cues with older toddlers to show how materials are used or help toddlers tell you what they want.
- Position the infant or toddler so that there is a clear view of the speaker. Lighting is important (have light illuminate the face of the speaker).

CAPITALIZE ON RESIDUAL AUDITORY ABILITIES

If a child can hear a particular sound, like a bell, use it when appropriate to get the child's attention. It is important to learn individual ways of capitalizing on residual hearing in order to foster independence and interaction with others. It is also important that the child becomes aware of those sounds that are within his capacity.

If the child has a hearing aid, the caregiver must know how to check it (daily) and change the battery as needed. The provider must also know how to put the aid in the child's ear. Many young children do not want to wear their aids, and a plan should be developed to help the child get used to wearing them consistently.

PLAY AND EXPLORATION

Support and facilitate interactions with toys and with peers. Use simple sign language with all children so that children are able to communicate with one another in another way.

Provide toys that are visually interesting that children can grasp, move, or create an effect by using. Modify toys and materials when necessary to make them more interesting or to create curiosity within the child.

Emotional or Behavioral Challenges

CLARITY, CONSISTENCY, AND PREDICTABILITY

Teach children clear and consistent limits. Model the behaviors you want to establish. Give children the words to express their feelings and acknowledge their right to have them. Make explanations brief and direct.

Provide "retreat spaces" for children to move in and out of on their own accord as needed. Some children need time alone to regroup.

Some toddlers are helped by having very concrete cues for transitions to alert them to what is going to happen next, such as ringing a bell to indicate when the play yard is available or pictures of the next activity (snack).

PROTECTION FROM NOISE AND CONFUSION

Reduced noise and movement are essential for children who are easily distracted or upset.

Be proactive. Observe interactions and behaviors closely to prevent provocations.

ENCOURAGING PLAY AND EXPLORATION

Be aware of individual stimulation thresholds. Some infants and toddlers do better with reduced stimulation and limited choices.

Most toddlers feel more secure when an adult is nearby, especially if they know they can depend on that adult to provide focus and control when needed. It's especially important to provide that control before a child damages materials or hurts another child.

Support, encourage, and facilitate interactions with toys and peers. Accept different levels of interaction as appropriate to each individual and provide limits for a child who needs them.

Developmental Disabilities

PACE

During caregiving routines and exploration periods, encourage the child to become involved. Explain what will happen and wait for the child to indicate in some way that the message was received. Give plenty of time for the child to do whatever he or she can to help. Allow the child to keep trying even when frustration arises, but be sensitive about what frustration level is too much.

PROVIDE FOR MOVEMENT

Familiarize the child with the environment. Provide tactile, auditory, and visual cues as guides. For the child who is not yet walking independently, provide opportunities for the child to move in whatever way he can.

Multi-Sensory Experiences

While multi-sensory experiences are important for all infants and toddlers, those with disabilities may need additional experiences and space that invites open-ended exploration and play.

Use language to help guide the infant or toddler in daily routines and activities. Use picture cues to show how materials are used or help toddlers tell you what they want if they don't have language or gestures to do it.

CAPITALIZE ON STRENGTHS

Support the child's successes. Give approval without distracting the child from his success or activity. Play/activity sequences may need to be broken down into smaller steps.

Provide for open-ended play and exploration. Be aware of safety considerations for a child who may be developing at a different rate (one who may still put things in his mouth).

All infants and toddlers need plenty of open-ended play and exploration, but some may not know what to do when provided with the opportunity in a safe and interesting environment. Help them by gently encouraging, being sure toys and materials are enticing and adapted to their abilities; give them some ideas about what to do with the toys and materials. Model, if necessary. Think about ways to stimulate curiosity to motivate children to explore.

Support, encourage, and facilitate interactions with toys and other children. Accept different levels of interaction as appropriate to each individual. Model appropriate interactions and behaviors. Describe interactions in simple terms.

ALLOW FOR EXTRA TIME AND REPEATED PRACTICE

Children learn best through practice and repetition. Children with developmental delays often need more opportunities to practice when learning new skills. In order for the skill to be mastered, the skill must be practiced many times and over several days or weeks. Provide encouragement to keep the child engaged while working toward mastery.

References

Child Development Resources (1993) *Special Care Curriculum and Trainer's Manual* PO Box 280 Norge VA 23127-0280 (757) 566-3300

Cook, R. E., Tessier. A. and Klein, M. D. (2000) *Adapting Early Childhood Curricula for Children in Inclusive Settings. Fifth Edition.* Upper Saddle River, NJ: Prentice Hall.

Cranor, L., and A. Kuschner, Editors; (1996) *Project Exceptional: A Guide for Recruiting and Training Childcare Providers to Serve Young Children with Disabilities*, Volume 2. Sacramento, California: California Department of Education.

Kuschner, A. and L. Cranor, and L. Brekken, Editors; (1996) *Project Exceptional: A Guide for Recruiting and Training Childcare Providers to Serve Young Children with Disabilities*, Volume 1. Sacramento, California: California Department of Education.

Questions about Reading 21

1. What do the letters in the SOUL technique stand for?

2. Notice the relatively passive nature of each part of the SOUL technique. Caregiving and teaching are usually considered to require activity on the part of the adult. Why do you think the SOUL technique is more passive than active?

3. What is interdependence? The authors state, "Independence and interdependence aren't opposites, but two sides of the same coin." What does that sentence mean to you?

4. What is one strategy you could use to help a toddler with a physical disability play and explore?

Part II

Important Forms

Organizations run on forms, and Infant-Toddler Care and Education Programs are no exception. Even organizations as small as family child care homes have some paperwork. In many locations the regulating and monitoring agencies have their own sets of forms that they require programs to use. What we are including here are samples of a variety of forms, but we added our own twist to them. For example, we replaced the traditional "mother's name" and "father's name" with the nongendered "parent's name" and "co-parent's name." We also tried to respect family privacy by giving more choices of what the person filling out the form can share. (See "Tell Us about Your Child.") Shortening some of the forms was also a goal. If you prefer a more traditional form upon entry, you are welcome to revise. Also, if you want a more formal form for finding out about the child's developmental progress and health information, please look at the one at the end of this section. We have included two forms there. The Physician's Report Form is required by some states. The one here is a sample.

Form 1

REGISTRATION FORM

Child's full name _____ Date of birth _____

Child's address _____

_____

Phone number _____

Parent or guardian information

Parent or guardian's name _____

Address _____

_____

Phone number _____

Place and hours of employment _____

Address _____

_____

Phone number _____

Co-parent or guardian's name _____

Address _____

_____

Phone number _____

Place of employment _____

Address _____

_____

Phone number _____

Persons authorized to pick up child _____

_____

_____

Persons who may not pick up child _____

_____

Form 2

TELL US ABOUT YOUR CHILD

Child's Name _____

What would you like us to call your child? _____

If you would like to, please tell us about the people who live in the home with the child. _____

_____

What should we know about your child's health? _____

_____

Does your child have any allergies? If yes, what is your child allergic to? _____

_____

What are the symptoms? _____

_____

How severe? Is there an antidote? _____

_____

Does your child take any medicine regularly, If yes, what? _____

_____

Do you have any concerns about your child that you want to tell us about? _____

_____

Does your child have a disability that has been diagnosed? _____

_____

Food

What do you want us to know about your child's feeding and eating patterns? _____

_____

How do you feed him or her? _____

_____

If your child is eating solid foods

- Are there any food restrictions? _____

- What are his or her likes, and dislikes? _____

  _____

- Does your child feed him or herself? _____

- How? Eat with fingers? Use a spoon? Use a fork? Use chopsticks? Drink out of a cup?

_____

Do you have any concerns about your child's feeding that you want us to know about? _____

_____

Do you have any feeding or mealtime rituals that you want to tell us about? _____

_____

Diapering and Toileting

If your child is in diapers, do you use cloth or disposable diapers? _____

If old enough

- how does your child indicate bathroom needs? _____

  _____

- What words does he or she use? _____

  _____

  _____

- Is he or she toilet trained? _____

  If not, what are your ideas about when and how to begin? _____

  _____

  _____

Sleeping and Napping

- What are your child's sleeping patterns? _____

  _____

- What do you want us to know about how you put your child to sleep? _____

  _____

- Does your child have a favorite toy or item he or she uses for comfort? _____

  _____

- Is there anything in particular that frightens your child? _____

  _____

  _____

- How do you comfort your child? _____

  _____

  _____

Home Language

What do you want us to know about who speaks what language in your home? _____

_____

If you had a choice, what language(s) would you want your child to hear and speak in the program?

_____

If your home language is not the language spoken in the program, do you want to teach us some key words in your language? _____

_____

What else do you want us to know about you and your child? _____

_____

_____

Form 3

IDENTIFICATION AND EMERGENCY FORM

Date _____

Child's name _____

Child's physician _____   Phone _____

Address _____

_____

Child's dentist _____   Phone _____

Address _____

_____

Parent's or guardian's name _____

Phone where you can be reached in an emergency _____

Please notify us if this changes (even temporarily)

Co-parent's name _____

Phone where this person can be reached in an emergency _____

Other people who can be called in case of emergency (Be sure to include people who will usually know where you are)

Name _____   Relationship to the child _____

Address_____

Phone number _____

Name _____   Relationship to the child _____

Address_____

Phone number _____

First Aid

In the event of an emergency, I authorize the staff to provide any first aid care deemed necessary for my child.

Signature/date _____

Emergency Care

In the event of an emergency in which I cannot be reached, the physician listed above and the local hospital are hereby authorized to provide any emergency care deemed necessary for my child.

Signature/date _____

Health Record Transfer

In the event of an emergency, I hereby authorize the transfer of my child's health record to the local hospital.

Signature/date _____

Form 4

INFANT FEEDING PLAN

Child's name _____

Birth date _____

Breast fed or formula? _____

Type of formula (if applicable) _____

_____

Does your infant eat solid foods? _____

If yes, what foods have already been introduced? _____

_____

_____

What plan do you have for introducing new foods? Please give details of what new foods you plan to introduce and when?

_____

_____

_____

_____

_____

_____

_____

_____

_____

Parent's signature _____

Caregiver's signature _____

Form 5

DAILY INFORMATION SHEET

Parent Section

Please give us any information that will help us to care for your child today:

Date _____

Child's name _____

Feedings _____

_____

Sleep _____

_____

Changes in elimination patterns _____

_____

Other _____

_____

Comments _____

_____

_____

Caregiver's Section

Dear Parent,

Here are how things went today

_____

_____

_____

_____

Feedings _____

Sleep _____

Diapers/toileting information _____

_____

Other _____

_____

Comments _____

_____

Form 6

SIGN-IN SHEET		
Date		
Child's name Write full name	Brought in by: Sign full name	Picked up by: Sign full name
1.	Time in_____	Time out _____
2.	Time in_____	Time out _____
3.	Time in_____	Time out _____
4.	Time in_____	Time out _____
5.	Time in_____	Time out _____
6.	Time in_____	Time out _____
7.	Time in_____	Time out _____
8.	Time in_____	Time out _____

Form 7

DIAPERING LOG		
Date		
Child changed	**Time**	**Comments**

Form 8

FEEDING LOG			
Child Fed	**Time**	**Description and Amount Consumed**	**Comments**

Form 9

ALLERGY NOTICE
To be prominently displayed

_____ is allergic to _____

CHILD'S NAME

_____ is allergic to _____

CHILD'S NAME

_____ is allergic to _____

CHILD'S NAME

_____ is allergic to _____

CHILD'S NAME

_____ is allergic to _____

CHILD'S NAME

_____ is allergic to _____

CHILD'S NAME

Form 10

SAMPLE EXPOSURE NOTICE

Note: The information contained below does not replace consultation with your physician if your child is sick.

Dear Parents:

On (date) _____ your child may have been exposed to the following disease:

_____

Onset of disease after exposure (how long): _____

The symptoms: _____

_____

This disease is spread by: _____

_____

It is contagious (when, for how long, at what stage): _____

_____

_____

It can be recognized/diagnosed by: _____

_____

Steps for treatment: _____

_____

_____

_____

Steps for preventsion: _____

_____

_____

_____

NOTE: *Keeping Kids Healthy* contains important facts about 26 communicable diseases most frequently encountered in child care programs.

Form 11

MEDICATION SCHEDULE				
Date	Name	Medication	Dose	Times

Form 12

INDIVIDUAL CHILD'S RECORD OF MEDICATIONS GIVEN

Dear Parent: Please complete this form and return along with medication.

Child's name _____

Illness _____

_____

Medication _____

_____

Dosage _____

_____

Dates to be given _____

Times to be given _____

I authorize the child care staff to administer the above medication from

_____ until _____

DATE   DATE

Parent's signature _____ Date _____

This part will be filled out by the caregiver:

Date	Medication Given	Dose	Time given	Given by

Form 13

INCIDENT LOG					
Date time	Name of child	Location	Type of incident	Action taken	Initials

Form 14

INCIDENT REPORT

Child's name _____

Date of incident _____ Time of incident _____

Description of incident _____

_____

_____

_____

Place incident occurred _____

_____

Description of incident (including any equipment or product involved) _____

_____

_____

Description of injury and body part involved _____

_____

Name of witnesses _____

Action taken _____

Was parent called? _____

Was anybody else called? _____

Was doctor called? _____

Corrective action needed to prevent such incidents from reoccurring. _____

_____

_____

_____

Additional information _____

_____

_____

_____

_____

_____

Signature _____ Date _____

Form 15

DOCUMENTATION OF CONCERN FOR A CHILD

Date _____

Child's name _____

Nature of Concern _____

_____

_____

_____

_____

_____

_____

_____

Detailed Observation _____

_____

_____

_____

_____

_____

_____

Proposed action to be taken _____

_____

_____

_____

_____

_____

_____

_____

Signature _____

Form 16

HOW ARE WE DOING?
FAMILY FEEDBACK FORM

Are we meeting your needs? Do you have any ideas about how we could do a better job?

_____

_____

Are we meeting your child's needs? Do you have any ideas about how we could do a better job?

_____

_____

Are our policies clear to you?

_____

_____

How do you feel about the communication between you and your child's caregiver or caregiving team?

_____

_____

How well do they respond to your concerns?

_____

_____

What are some things you would like them to know to better understand you and your child?

_____

_____

How do you feel about the information you get about your child's day?

_____

_____

Are there things that you would like to see included in your child's day that aren't there now?

_____

_____

Do you think the program is respectful of diversity?

_____

_____

What else do you want to tell us?

_____

_____

Form 17

DEVELOPMENTAL HEALTH HISTORY

Child's name _____   Birth date _____/_____/_____
                (Last)   (First)

Nickname _____

Physical Health

What health problems has your child had in the past? _____

_____

_____

_____

What health problems does your child have now? _____

_____

_____

Other than what you listed above, does your child have any allergies? If so, to what?_____

_____

_____

How severe? _____

_____

Does your child take any medicine regularly? If so, what? _____

_____

Has your child ever been hospitalized? if so, when and why? _____

_____

_____

Does your child have any recurring chronic illness or health problem (such as asthma or frequent earaches)? _____

_____

Does your child have a disability that has been diagnosed (such as cerebral palsy, seizure disorder, developmental delay)? _____

_____

Do you have any other concerns about your child's health?_____

_____

_____

_____

Development (compared with other children this age)

Does your child have any problems with talking or making sounds? Please explain. _____

_____

Does your child have any problems with walking, running, or moving? Please explain. _____

_____

Does your child have any problems seeing? Please explain._____

_____

_____

Does your child have any problems using her or his hands (such as with puzzles, drawing, small building pieces)? Please explain. _____

_____

_____

Daily living

What is your child's typical eating pattern? _____

_____

_____

Write N/A (non applicable) if your child is too young for the following questions to apply:

What foods does your child like? _____

Dislike? _____

How well does your child use table utensils (cup, fork, spoon)?_____

_____

How does your child indicate bathroom needs? Word(s) for *urination:* _____

Word(s) for *bowel movement:* _____

Special words for body parts: _____

What are your child's regular bladder and bowel patterns? Do you want us to follow a particular plan for toilet training? _____

_____

For toddlers, please describe the use of diapers or toileting equipment at home (such as a potty, toilet seat adapter)_____

_____

What are your child's regular sleeping patterns?

Awakes at _____   Naps at _____   Goes to bed at _____

What help does your child need to get dressed? _____

_____

Social relationships/play

What ages are your child's most frequent playmates? _____

Is your child friendly? _____ Aggressive? _____ Shy? _____ Withdrawn? _____

Does your child play well alone? _____

_____

What is your child's favorite toy? _____

_____

What frightens your child? (Circle all that apply.) Animals? Rough children? Loud noises? The dark? Storms? Anything else? _____

_____

Who does most of the disciplining? _____

_____

What is the best way to discipline your child? _____

_____

_____

With which adults does your child have frequent contact? _____

_____

How do you comfort your child? _____

_____

Does your child use a special comforting item (such as a blanket, stuffed animal, doll)? _____

_____

_____

Parent's signature _____

Date _____

Form 18

PHYSICIAN'S REPORT FORM—DAY CARE CENTERS

STATE OF CALIFORNIA HEALTH AND HUMAN SERVICES AGENCY   DEPARTMENT OF SOCIAL SERVICES COMMUNITY CARE LICENSING

PHYSICIAN'S REPORT—CHILD CARE CENTERS

(CHILD'S PRE-ADMISSION HEALTH EVALUATION)

PART A—PARENT'S CONSENT (TO BE COMPLETED BY PARENT)

_____, born _____ is being studied for readiness to enter
(NAME OF CHILD)   (DATE OF BIRTH)

_____. The Child Care Center/School provides a program which extends from _____
(NAME OF CHILD CARE CENTER/SCHOOL)

a.m./p.m. to _____ a.m./p.m. _____ days a week.

Please provide a report on above-named child using the form below. I hereby authorize release of medical information contained in this report to the above-named Child Care Center.

_____   _____
(SIGNATURE OF PARENT, GUARDIAN OR CHILD'S AUTHORIZED REPRESENTATIVE)   (TODAY'S DATE)

PART B—PHYSICIAN'S REPORT (TO BE COMPLETED BY PHYSICIAN)

Problems of which you should be aware:

Hearing:	Allergies: medicine:
Vision:	Insect stings:
Developmental:	Food:
Language/Speech:	Asthma:
	Other:

Other (including behavioral concerns):

Comments/Explanations

MEDICATION PRESCRIBED/SPECIAL, ROUTINES/RESTRICTIONS FOR THE CHILD: _____

IMMUNIZATION HISTORY: (Fill out or enclose California Immunization Record, PM-298.)

VACCINE		DATE EACH DOSE WAS GIVEN				
		1st	2nd	3rd	4th	5th
POLIO	(OPV OR IPV)	/ /	/ /	/ /	/ /	/ /
DTP/DTEP/ DT/DD	(DIPTHERIA, TETANUS AND [ACELLULAR] PERTUSSIS OR TETANUS AND DIPHTHERIA ONLY)	/ /	/ /	/ /	/ /	/ /
MMR	(MIEASLES, MUMPS, AND RUBELLA)	/ /	/ /	/ /	/ /	/ /
HIB MENINGITIS	(REQUIRED FOR CHILD CARE ONLY) (HAEMOPHILUS B)	/ /	/ /	/ /	/ /	/ /
HEPATITIS B		/ /	/ /	/ /	/ /	/ /
VARICELLA	(NOT REQUIRED) (CHICKENPOX)	/ /	/ /	/ /	/ /	/ /

> **SCREENING OF TB RISK FACTORS** (listing on reverse side)
> ❑ Risk factors not present; TB skin test not required.
> ❑ Risk factors present; Mentoux TB skin test performed (unless previous positive skin test documented).
> ____ Communicable TB disease not present.

I have ❑   have not ❑   reviewed the above information with the parent/guardian.

Physician: _____   Date of Physical Exam: _____

Address: _____   Date This Form Completed: _____

Telephone: _____   Signature: _____

❑ Physician   ❑ Physician's Assistant   ❑ Nurse Practitioner

Part III

Communicating with Parents

Upon starting an infant-toddler care and education program, each family should receive a parent handbook that tells them what to expect, including enrollment information, policies and procedures, as well as their rights and responsibilities. This section contains the outline of a sample parent handbook and sample letters and notices that could go into it.

Parent Handbook

It's important to put information in writing. Some parent handbooks are real books with many pages. Others are slim pamphlets. They are usually evolving; as the program and parents change, they need to be regularly updated. This is a bare outline of what can be included in a parent handbook. Obviously each handbook must be tailored to the specific program.

Outline

Here's a sample of what a parent handbook can contain.

Welcome statement

Philosophy statement

Program organization

Information about staff members

Admission and enrollment procedures

Fees (if any)

Health policies and practices

Nutrition plan

Communication between families and the program, such as conferences

Disaster policy, plans, and preparedness

Guidance and discipline policies

Statement about the legal mandate to report suspected abuse

Antibias and inclusion policies

PLEASANT VALLEY INFANT CENTER

Street Address

City, State and Zipcode

Telephone number

Dear Parents and Family Members,

Welcome to the Pleasant Valley Infant Center. We are pleased to have you and your child as part of our program. We want you to feel welcome and we will do everything we can to make your child feel at home. We look forward to getting to know you and your child.

We believe in working in collaboration with parents and family members so that we can become your partner in the care and education of your child. You are welcome to visit any time, either in the room with your child or in our observation room. We invite your feedback and suggestions on how to make the program work even better for you and your child. Please feel free to bring any of your questions or concerns to the caregivers or director.

If you have time and care to participate beyond observing, we have information available to explain the many ways you can get involved at the level where you are most comfortable. For example, we can use you on the advisory board, as a volunteer in the infant center, or even in the office. We also need maintenance and repair work periodically, and appreciate when family members help out.

Your child's primary caregiver is Shawna and her partner in the infant room is Eduardo, so your child will get to know both of the teachers, though Shawna will be the teacher who will be most connected to your child.

Further information about our philosophy, goals, policies, and practices are included in the Parent/Family Handbook. A staff directory is also included. Please read the "What to Bring" list for your child's first day in the program.

Again, we welcome you to our program and hope your time here meets your goals and expectations.

Sincerely,

The Director and Staff

Pleasant Valley Infant Center

WHAT TO BRING

- **Diapers.**

- **Change of clothes** labeled with child's name inside. It is very important to keep a change of clothes here at the center for your child. If your child's clothes become wet or soiled, we will put them in their cubby in a plastic bag for you to take home and wash. When this happens, you need to bring another change of clothes the following day.

- **Blanket** to keep at the center, especially if your child has an attachment to a particular type of blanket.

- **Bottle** from home if you do not want to use ours. Our dishwasher has a special sterilization cycle, so it safe to use our center bottles, if you want.

- **A warm jacket** or sweatshirt to play outside during the cool months.

- **Clothing suitable for water play** during the warm months.

- **Sunscreen** for the warm months. You must sign a permission form for us to be able to apply sunscreen. You may wish to apply it yourself before bringing your child to the center.

- **A hat** for sunny days.

Shoes and slippers if your child is walking. Inside, children go barefoot or wear slippers, but they need shoes for outside to protect their feet.

Thank you,

The Infant Room Staff

PHILOSOPHY STATEMENT

We aim to provide a nurturing, secure, consistent, and home-like environment for the infants and toddlers in our program. We do this by creating a primary caregiver system within small groups. We believe in continuity of care and education, so children become attached to their primary caregivers and keep the same one for as long as possible—ideally for the length of enrollment.

We are an inclusion program that integrates children with disabilities and other challenges into the group of typically developing children. Individualized care and education is another goal. We believe that this will come about when we respect individual, family, and cultural values and beliefs by incorporating them into our daily routines to the extent possible. We individualize feeding, diapering, napping, and socialization. For example, we pay attention to the home feeding and sleeping approaches and rituals. We find out the child's favorite activities and the environmental characteristics at home, and we try to incorporate at least some of these into our center's environment and routines so the child feels consistency between home and the center.

We help to ease transitions and turn them into positive experiences. Transitions include: separation from parent, separation from caregivers at the center, moving from inside play to outside and back, transitions to mealtime, going to sleep and waking up, and going home at the end of the day.

We provide activities of all sorts, which fall into two basic categories: 1. The essential activities of daily living (feeding, diapering, etc.) during which the primary and sometimes secondary caregiver are working one-on-one with the child and focused on building a secure relationship. These activities are considered vital to the learning process and are carried out by caregivers trained to be gentle, respectful, and responsive, and to involve the child so he or she learns to be cooperative from the beginning of life. 2. Experiences that respond to the child's individual interests and involve the senses, as well as supporting self-help skills, problem-solving skills, and motor development. These experiences encourage creativity and enhance cognitive development as well as socialization. These occur throughout every day and, along with the essential activities of daily living, provide opportunities for children's language development in the home language and also in English, if the home language is other than English.

Progress is monitored and documented throughout the year and includes written observations, check lists, and anecdotal records, as well as documentation through photographs and video. Information from parents (through forms and conferences) is also part of the data and documentation.

DAILY SCHEDULE

7:30	Center opens

Note: Times between opening and closing are approximate

8:00-9:30	Breakfast for the children who eat as a group
9:00-10:50	Free play (includes a rich environment set up indoors and outside so children have a variety of experiences that contribute to their individual learning, development, and socialization. Note, free play runs throughout the day for those children who are not involved in feeding, diapering, or napping.)
9:00-11:30	Morning bottles / spoon feeding / napping/ diapering/ as needed
10:50-11:10	Cleanup and preparation for lunch
11:15-11:45	Lunch for the children who eat as a group
12:00-2:30	Afternoon bottles / spoon feeding / napping/ diapering/ as needed
2:30-2:45	Afternoon snack for children who eat as a group
2:30-4:30	Diapering / bottles as needed
1:30-5:00	Free play (includes a rich environment set up indoors and outside so children have a variety of experiences that contribute to their individual learning, development, and socialization. Note, free play runs throughout the day for those children who are not involved in feeding, diapering, or napping.)
5:00	Center closes

Part IV

Observation

Observation Guidelines
Video Observations

Observation Guidelines

This last section gives tips and hints about observing infants and toddlers. Observation is an important part of a caregiver's job, and occurs every minute of every day. How else is the caregiver to know what each child needs minute to minute, as well as how to respond to and interact with the child? Through observation, caregivers can change the mode of interaction to fit each child, or discover how the environment is working. Observation is the key to implementing curriculum. Every part of the program is built on observation. Children whose caregivers observe them closely enough to know them well feel more secure. The message throughout the book *Infants, Toddlers, and Caregivers* is "pay attention!" This section gives some hints about how to pay attention to where you are and who is there with you.

Observation is more than just watching. It is paying attention with all one's senses in order to understand. It is making the invisible visible and also being aware of what's not happening as well as what is. This kind of understanding comes through analyzing and interpreting what you perceive. Skilled observers learn to see with "ethnographic eyes."

Besides the informal ongoing observations, caregivers also make more formal ones on occasion, especially when they want to find out something that they can't just casually discover. Some of these observations must occur over time. Some forms these observations take are quick notes, lengthier notes, and check lists. The notes can be made on the spot or written down later from memory. Writing is required because if caregivers don't keep records of what they observe, they forget. Memory alone can't hold all the details needed. Written records are useful in many ways. One way is by reviewing them over a period of time, sometimes patterns emerge that wouldn't show otherwise.

To be truly representative, observations must occur in a variety of settings, situations, and times of day. There's no other way to truly understand either individuals or groups. The same is true of observing families. Remember that you can't really know a family if you see them only at the worst time of the day—when they are saying good-bye and hurrying away or when they come back tired and ready to go home and prepare the next meal.

For record keeping purposes it is important to always write down the date and time of an observation, as well as the name and age of child, unless it is part of the observation record when the child was born. It can help to also include the setting and additional information such as the specific circumstance. Observing the first day back from a vacation is different from observing the last day before a vacation. Be respectful of the individual's feelings and don't be intrusive. It can be uncomfortable to feel like one is under a microscope.

The data you gather through observations should be detailed and objective. Of course, you also need to give interpretation to that objective data. You see the child is rubbing her eyes. You may not know why for sure, but in looking at the child and the context you might be able to guess. Is this a baby who always takes a nap at this time of day? Is this a toddler who is sitting in the sandbox? Have you noticed the redness in this child's eyes and you suspect an infection? The eye rubbing is the data. The guess as to its meaning, or why it is happening, is your interpretation. Both are important, but keep them separate. Be aware of which is which.

The goal is to be objective, but that doesn't mean we can ever step out of our own skin. The observer is always part of the picture. Become aware of the effects you are having on what and whom you are observing. Also observe the effects on you of what you see. Notice sore areas and hot spots that the actions of others touch in you. Notice the part of you that is wanting to judge what you are seeing. Notice the part of you that is quick to jump to conclusions. Be aware that those conclusions may be based on false assumptions. Although you try to gather objective data through observations, you can't leave yourself out of it. Separate the objective and subjective. If the subjective in the form of judgments, assumptions, and feelings keeps getting in the way, write it down and acknowledge that it is subjective. Then focus on turning to a more objective mode where you observe what's really happening and interpret it without all the personal issues you've acknowledged and put away.

Observation is a useful tool in many ways. Through observing children you learn about their developmental stage, as well as their uniqueness—their likes and dislikes, behavior patterns, how they interact with others and the world around them. You can get insights on how to intervene to enhance the child's learning process. A good observer can even begin to see the world from other perspectives.

Video Observations

This section lets you experiment with various ways of focusing on and recording behavior. Each Video Observation corresponds with a video clip at the Online Learning Center and expands beyond the Video Observation feature in each chapter of your textbook. You can use these Video Observations to practice various forms of observation and hone your observation skills.

Chapter 1: Principles, Practice, and Curriculum

OLC Video Observation 1: Baby Crying

This clip illustrates some of the principles of Chapter 1. Read or review the chapter before doing this observation. When you watch the clip, look for at least one thing that relates to one of the principles in Chapter 1.

OBSERVATION AND REFLECTION

Directions: Watch the clip from beginning to end. It's a very short segment. Then think back to what you observed. Write down as much as you remember, giving as many details as possible. Try to fill space below if you can. When you finish writing, watch the video again and go back and add more details. Change what you wrote (if needed). Continue on another sheet of paper if you fill up this one. Then write one sentence at the bottom of your observations saying what you learned by doing it.

Chapter 2: Infant-Toddler Education

OLC Video Observation 2: Toddler Playing with a Tube and Ball

In this clip, you are looking at an example of the kinds of educational experiences that children of this age choose for themselves. Read or review the section on problem solving in Chapter 2 in preparation for doing this observation.

RUNNING RECORD OBSERVATION

Directions: The idea of a running record observation is to take quick notes on what you are seeing, including as many details as possible. Then write up your observation in the sequence in which it unfolded. Use complete sentences and paragraphs. What you write should be objective: only what you saw. Don't take short-cuts like "the child played with the ball and tube." Describe his actions in the most minute detail possible and include such things as body posture and movement, facial expressions, and other details that you can actually see. Use this page to take notes and write up your running record observation on a separate sheet of paper.

Chapter 3: Caregiving as Curriculum

OLC Video Observation 3: Children Feeding Themselves

Mealtimes are part of the curriculum. See if writing anecdotal records as in the instructions below helps you see the curriculum aspects of this scene.

ANECDOTAL RECORDS

Directions: Watch this clip without writing anything down. Now give one child a name and then write down as much as you can remember about that child. Did anything particularly stand out in your memory? Then give another child a name and write down as much as you can remember about that child. Again, think about what stood out in your memory.

Child 1 Name_____

Child 2 Name _____

What you just wrote were two anecdotal records, which are short records written after the fact about anything that stood out in your mind about particular children.

Self-reflection: Did you find you were more attracted to one of the children than the other? If yes, what attracted you? Was it easier to remember something about the one that attracted you or the one who didn't? (Use an additional sheet if you need more room.)

Chapter 4: Play as Curriculum

OLC Video Observation 4: Toddlers Playing Outside

This clip is an illustration of toddler play.

ANECDOTAL RECORDS

Directions: Watch this clip without writing anything down. Now give one child a name and then write down as much as you can remember about that child. Did anything particularly stand out in your memory? Then give the other child a name and write down as much as you can remember about that child. Again, think about what stood out in your memory.

Child 1 Name _____

Child 2 Name _____

Chapter 5: Attachment

OLC Video Observation 5: Toddler "Checking In" while Playing with Chairs

Read or review Chapter 5 to recall how attachment shows up in specific behaviors.

OBSERVING FOR SOMETHING SPECIFIC

Directions: Watch for a sign of attachment behavior in this clip. Write it down in as much detail as you can in the space below. NOTE: Because this is a video clip, not a real-life observation, the specific behavior you will be looking for is going to occur in the minute or so you are observing the clip, so you are guaranteed to find it. In real life you might have to observe for a much longer time and might never see the behavior you are looking for.

What attachment behavior(s) did you see? Record here what you observed:

Chapter 6: Perception

OLC Video Observation 6: Boy Exploring Toy Car using Touch and Sound

Chapter 6 discusses perception, but perception is something that goes on inside the brain and can't be seen except in behaviors. One never really knows what someone else perceives. One can only guess.

RUNNING RECORD OBSERVATION

Directions: Observe the boy and take notes on what you see. Write those notes up as a running record observation as in the Video Observation for Chapter 2. Then answer the question below.

Although you can't know what the child is perceiving, still you can try interpreting his behavior in terms of what you think he is perceiving. Write about what seems to be coming in through his ears and sense of touch. Are any other senses involved?

Chapter 7: Motor Skills

OLC Video Observation 7: Children Climbing Stairs

This clip is your perfect chance to closely observe motor skills in ways that go beyond the information in Chapter 7.

OBSERVE FOR THE SMALLEST DETAILS

Directions: The point of this observation is to hone your skills for noticing details. Observe the clip once without writing. Watch for the movements, balance, posture, facial expressions. Now observe again and write notes. Observe still again and fill out your notes further. Continue to observe until you no longer see anything new. Then write up a running record observation describing in the most minute detail what you saw. Be specific and objective throughout.

Chapter 8: Cognition

OLC Video Observation 8: Father Diapering Toddler

You probably expected some activity that more obviously related to cognition. This clip was intentionally selected to make the point that caregiving is curriculum and it not only relates to social-emotional development, but to cognitive development as well.

OBSERVING INTERACTIONS

Directions: Up until now you've been asked to observe one person at a time. This time the focus is on the interaction between the father and his son. Do a running record observation (directions in the Video Observation for Chapter 2 on page 162) and interpret what you see in terms of cognition.

Chapter 9: Language

OLC Video Observation 9: Children Eating at Table with Caregiver

It is said that language is caught, not taught. Observe this clip for how children are "catching" language from the caregiver.

OBSERVATION FOCUSED ON LANGUAGE

Directions: Observe this clip and write down what the caregiver says and does. Go back and observe again and write down specific child responses each time the caregiver talks. You can watch as many times as you want, filling out your observation with more details each time. Write this up at the end as a running record observation (as in the directions in the Video Observation for Chapter 2 on page 162.)

Chapter 10: Emotions

OLC Video Observation 10: Child Trying to get her Turn in a Swing

This clip shows a child exhibiting feelings. The observer sometimes feels emotional watching it.

SELF OBSERVATION

Directions: Watch the clip and note your own feelings. Use the space below to write down a self-reflection of what went on inside you as you watched the clip. The point is that observations should be objective and feelings can get in the way of objectivity. By becoming aware of one's reactions and writing them down you can then consciously put them aside and write objective descriptions and interpretations.

Chapter 11: Social Skills

OLC Video Observation 11: Girls Playing Together

Although toddlers are known for their parallel play, during which they don't interact with each other, the two girls in this clip are obviously interacting.

OBSERVING THE DETAILS OF AN INTERACTION

Directions: Watch the whole clip once. Then watch it again, making notes on what happens during the brief periods of interaction. Write down facial expressions, body movements, sounds (if any) and whatever else you observe. Then write up descriptions of each interaction. Be extremely detailed and specific in your descriptions.

Chapter 12: The Physical Environment

OLC Video Observation 12: Feeding Routine

This clip illustrates how the environment influences behavior, as explained in Chapter 12.

OBSERVING DETAILS OF THE ENVIRONMENT

Directions: Review Chapter 1 so you have the philosophy of your textbook firmly in your mind as you watch this clip. Record the environmental features that relate to this philosophy. Then explain how each feature influences the child's behavior based on what you observe in the clip.

Chapter 13: The Social Environment

OLC Video Observation 13: Child in Sandbox (Redirection)

Review the section on discipline in Chapter 13 of your textbook to reacquaint yourself with redirection

---

OBSERVING AN ADULT REDIRECTING A CHILD'S BEHAVIOR

Directions: Write here exactly what you observe the adult doing and the behaviors of the child in response to the adult behaviors. Use careful detail in your description.

Chapter 14: Adult Relations in Infant-Toddler Care and Education Programs

OLC Video Observation 14: Girl Crawling through Low Window (Parent Ed Program)

This clip shows an example of a program focused on parent education. Think about what you learned in Chapter 14 as you watch the clip.

OBSERVING A PARENT'S BEHAVIORS

Directions: Although the child is the centerpiece of this clip, observe the father's behaviors in response to her. Note details of his movements, posture, facial expressions, and sounds. Notice how he reacts to the teacher's voice complimenting him on his ability to let his baby solve her own problem. Write up your observation and at the end, write what you learned by doing it.